The Brockport Physical Fitness Test Manual

The Brockport Physical Fitness Test Manual

Joseph P. Winnick, EdD
Francis X. Short, PED

State University of New York
College at Brockport

Human Kinetics

Library of Congress Cataloging-in-Publication Data

Winnick, Joseph P.
   The Brockport physical fitness test manual / Joseph P. Winnick,
Francis X. Short.
        p.   cm.
   Includes bibliographical references and index.
   ISBN 0-7360-0021-6
   1. Physical fitness for children--Testing--Handbooks, manuals,
etc.   2. Exercise therapy for children--Handbooks, manuals, etc.
3. Handicapped children--Development--Handbooks, manuals, etc.
I. Short, Francis Xavier, 1950-   . II. Title.
RJ138.W55   1999
613.7'042'0287--dc21   98-42143
                                                                    CIP

ISBN: 0-7360-0021-6

Acquisitions Editor: Michael S. Bahrke, PhD; **Developmental Editor:** Kristine Enderle; **Assistant Editor:** Amy Flaig; **Copyeditor:** Karen Bojda; **Proofreader:** Sarah Wiseman; **Indexer:** Joan Griffitts; **Graphic Designer**: Fred Starbird; **Graphic Artist:** Denise Lowry; **Cover Designer:** Jack Davis; **Illustrator:** Tim Offenstein; **Printer:** United Graphics

Printed in the United States of America   10   9   8   7   6   5   4   3

Human Kinetics
Web site: www.HumanKinetics.com

United States: Human Kinetics, P.O. Box 5076, Champaign, IL 61825-5076
800-747-4457
e-mail: humank@hkusa.com

Canada: Human Kinetics, 475 Devonshire Road, Unit 100, Windsor, ON N8Y 2L5
800-465-7301 (in Canada only)
e-mail: orders@hkcanada.com

Europe: Human Kinetics, 107 Bradford Road, Stanningley
Leeds LS28 6AT, United Kingdom
+44 (0) 113 255 5665
e-mail: hk@hkeurope.com

Australia: Human Kinetics, 57A Price Avenue, Lower Mitcham, South Australia 5062
08 8277 1555
e-mail: liaw@hkaustralia.com

New Zealand: Human Kinetics, Division of Sports Distributors NZ Ltd.
P.O. Box 300 226 Albany, North Shore City, Auckland
0064 9 448 1207
e-mail: info@humankinetics.co.nz

CONTENTS

Chapter 5 Test Administration and Test Items   71

Chapter 6 Testing Youngsters With Severe Disabilities   129

Appendix A Body Mass Index Chart   133

Appendix B Purchasing and Constructing
Unique Testing Supplies   135

Appendix C Software Installation Instructions   141

PREFACE

In 1993 the U.S. Department of Education funded Project Target, a research study designed primarily to develop a health-related, criterion-referenced physical fitness test for youngsters ages 10 to 17 with disabilities. Project Target was centered at the State University of New York, College at Brockport, directed by Joseph P. Winnick, and coordinated by Francis X. Short. An important goal of the project was to develop standards for the attainment of healthful living through physical fitness and to enhance the development of health-related fitness of youngsters with disabilities.

The test that was developed through Project Target has been designated the Brockport Physical Fitness Test (BPFT). This manual presents information necessary to understand the test, administer test items, and interpret the results of testing. Information regarding validity and reliability is summarized in this manual; detailed information can be found in *The Fitness Challenge: Software for the Brockport Physical Fitness Test* (Short & Winnick, 1999; Winnick & Short, 1998).

The first chapter of this test manual includes an introduction and identifies, defines, and classifies target populations. It is important that all testers become familiar with this information.

The second chapter presents information about the conceptual framework for the test. Physical activity, health, and health-related physical fitness are discussed, and their relationships for the purposes of the BPFT are presented. A personalized approach to physical fitness testing is described. This personalized approach includes identifying health-related concerns, creating a desired physical fitness profile that emerges from the health-related concerns identified, selecting the components of physical fitness to be measured, identifying test items that measure the components of physical fitness, and selecting and applying health-related standards to evaluate physical fitness.

The third chapter presents our recommendations for using the BPFT. Three alternatives for using the test are presented: using only existing test items and standards in the BPFT, adjusting the BPFT for youngsters with disabilities, and combining the BPFT with other tests for a general (nondisabled) population or with other disability-specific tests. The final section of this chapter deals briefly with development of an individualized education program.

The fourth chapter of this test manual presents health-related, criterion-referenced test selection guides and standards for assessing physical fitness. This information is presented in tables that identify health-related parameters for youngsters in the general population and those with specific disabilities.

The fifth chapter of the test manual includes general recommendations for test administration and specific instructions for administering test items. All 27 test items that make up the BPFT are presented, although the number of test items administered to each individual generally falls between 4 and 6. The object of test items, a description of how they are to be administered, the equipment needed, ways of scoring, trials required, test modifications, and suggestions for test administration are presented. Test items are presented within categories reflecting the components of physical fitness used in the study: aerobic functioning, body composition, and musculoskeletal functioning, including muscular strength and endurance and flexibility or range of motion.

The sixth chapter deals with testing the physical fitness of youngsters with severe disabilities. During the design of the BPFT, it became obvious that not all disabilities or levels of function could be accommodated through a single physical fitness test. The BPFT is appropriate for most youngsters with disabilities and unique physical fitness needs; however, it may not be appropriate for youngsters with severe disabilities. Two orientations related to the measurement of physical fitness or physical activity of individuals with severe disabilities are offered: one related to task analysis and the other to the measurement of physical activity.

The appendixes at the end of this test manual include a table of body mass index and an appendix about purchasing and constructing unique equipment. A glossary of terms and identification of the many contributors to the project are also provided.

In presenting the BPFT we wish to emphasize that we consider this to be a point of departure for a valid and reliable test of physical fitness. There is little question that the test items and standards suggested in this manual will require continued scrutiny and study. Information on the development and establishment of the BPFT has been presented in a detailed technical manual available from *The Fitness Challege: Software for the Brockport Physical Fitness Test* (Short & Winnick, 1999) and/or the authors. The authors may be contacted at the Department of Physical Education and Sport, State University of New York, College at Brockport, Brockport, N.Y. 14420. The technical manual of *The Fitness Challenge: Software for the Brockport Physical Fitness Test* (Short & Winnick, 1999) should be studied thoroughly for a full understanding of the rationale for the test and the basis for the test items and standards recommended.

ACKNOWLEDGMENTS

The Brockport Physical Fitness Test was developed with the help of a diverse group of people and institutions as a part of Project Target. The project could not have been completed without the cooperation of many individuals, schools, and agencies throughout the United States. The project did not have the resources to fully compensate individuals for their contributions. Those who helped did so believing that their efforts would result in a project that would be helpful in enhancing the health-related fitness of individuals with disabilities. The names of individuals and educational institutions that made contributions to the project appear at the end of this manual. We extend deep gratitude to these people and organizations. Our thanks also are given to the many parents and youngsters who volunteered their time and effort for testing purposes. They also believed that the project would bring benefits to youngsters with disabilities.

Some individuals made extraordinary contributions to this project. At the forefront of these contributors was the Project Target Advisory Committee. The individuals on the advisory board provided overall guidance to Project Target in general and to the development of this test manual in particular. The committee also served as a panel of experts. The outstanding advisory committee included Kirk J. Cureton, PhD, University of Georgia; Harold W. Kohl, PhD, Baylor Sports Medicine Institute; Kenneth Richter, DO, medical director, United States Cerebral Palsy Athletic Association; James H. Rimmer, PhD, Northern Illinois University; Margaret Jo Safrit, PhD, American University; Roy J. Shephard, MD, PhD, DPE, University of Toronto; and Julian U. Stein, EdD, George Mason University (retired).

Paul Surburg at Indiana University deserves special recognition. Paul gave continued advice in the development of test items and standards associated with flexibility and range of motion. Special recognition is also extended to Bo Fernhall at George Washington University. Bo gave the project much insight in the area of aerobic fitness for individuals with disabilities and conducted some valuable research for the development of the BPFT. Patrick DiRocco of the University of Wisconsin at La Crosse gave valuable input on test items related to musculoskeletal functioning.

Special appreciation is extended to Pam Maryjanowski, who is associated with the Empire State Games for the Physically Challenged. Pam was particularly helpful in gaining access to subjects for the study. Two other individuals who also made the project's data collection possible were Paul Ponchillia, Western Michigan University, and Sister Seraphine Herbst, director of the School of the Holy Childhood in Rochester, New York. Arnie Epstein and Bob Lewis from the New York City Public Schools were extremely helpful in organizing data collection efforts in that school district. Each of these people very willingly and ably contributed to data collection efforts that were important for the development of the BPFT.

One important function in the development of standards for the BPFT was to test a general (nondisabled) population of youngsters. The Brockport Central

School District was very important in this regard. Over 900 subjects were tested in the district, and these data served as a source for the development of health-related, criterion-referenced physical fitness standards. Thanks are given to the administrators of the school district and the 15 physical education teachers associated with the district who cooperated and gave much help when their students were tested.

Gratitude is expressed to Richard Incardona for assisting in the preparation of the art. This manuscript was typed repeatedly by enthusiastic assistants Melissa Zurlo and Paul Plavetzki. Thanks also are given to many individuals who posed for pictures or sketches in the manual, including Kevin Wexler, Kelda DePrez, Lori Volding, Travis Phillips, Tucker Short, and Stephanie White. Several youngsters with disabilities also posed for pictures.

Thanks are extended to the professional organizations that endorsed and cooperated with the project. The American Alliance for Health, Physical Education, Recreation and Dance (AAHPERD) and the National Consortium for Physical Education and Recreation for Individuals with Disabilities (NCPERID) supported the original proposal for funding the project and provided opportunities for several presentations regarding the BPFT at professional meetings. Gratitude is extended to the Cooper Institute for Aerobic Research in Dallas, Texas. Their work with *FITNESSGRAM* served as a prototype for the BPFT. Several test items and standards from *FITNESSGRAM* are used by the BPFT enhancing a link between the two tests.

1

INTRODUCTION

The Brockport Physical Fitness Test (BPFT) is a health-related, criterion-referenced test of fitness. The term *health-related* is used to distinguish objectives of this test battery from one that might be more appropriately related to skill or physical performance. The phrase *criterion-referenced* conveys that the standards for evaluation are based on values believed to have some significance for an individual's health. Criterion-referenced standards can be established in a number of ways, including research findings, logic, expert opinion, and norm-referenced data (e.g., averages, percentiles).

In the mid-1990s, the American Alliance for Health, Physical Education, Recreation and Dance (AAHPERD) adopted the Prudential *FITNESSGRAM* (Cooper Institute for Aerobics Research, 1992) as its recommended health-related criterion-referenced test of physical fitness. Although the Prudential *FITNESSGRAM* manual contains a section on special populations, different or modified test items or standards were not presented in any systemic way for youngsters with specific disabilities.

From 1993 to 1998 the State University of New York, College at Brockport, was funded by the Office of Special Education and Rehabilitative Services, U.S. Department of Education, as a part of Project Target to develop a health-related, criterion-referenced physical fitness test for youngsters ages 10 to 17 with disabilities. A key element of the project was to develop standards that would provide targets for the attainment of health-related physical fitness. In addition, Project Target was funded to develop an educational component that would enhance the development of health-related fitness of youngsters with disabilities. The population targeted in this project included youngsters with mental retardation, spinal cord injury, cerebral palsy, blindness, congenital anomalies, and amputations. Although the project targeted these disabilities, its result contributed to a process of physical fitness testing that can be used for youngsters with other disabilities and youngsters in the general population. A total of 1,542 youngsters with and without disabilities were tested, and data from several projects including thousands of youngsters were analyzed as a part of Project Target. The Brockport Physical Fitness Test is the result of activities of Project Target.

A number of unique elements are associated with the BPFT. First, it represents an initial attempt to apply a health-related, criterion-referenced fitness approach to youngsters with disabilities. Second, it recognizes the individualized nature of fitness testing and encourages a personalized approach based on health-related needs and a desired fitness profile. Third, in an effort to provide options for test administrators to personalize testing, the battery includes several different fitness test items from which to choose. A complete battery for one individual generally includes four to six items. Finally, some of the test items are new (or at least nontraditional) and are designed to include a larger number of youngsters in the testing program than previously possible.

As fitness testing manuals go, this one is pretty thick. Many of the pages are dedicated to directions for individual test items found in chapter 5. Testers should also become familiar with the earlier material, however. Understanding the rationale for the test (along with its strengths and weaknesses) is important in interpreting results.

TEST CONSTRUCTION

There are 27 test items associated with the BPFT. However, generally only four to six items are needed to assess the health-related physical fitness of a particular youngster. As one might expect, considerable study was undertaken to determine the test items to be recommended in the test and the standards that would be used to evaluate physical fitness.

The process developed to select test items and standards for youngsters reflects the personalized approach described in detail in chapter 2. The steps include identifying and selecting health-related concerns of importance for a youngster, establishing a desired personalized fitness profile, selecting components and subcomponents of physical fitness to assess, selecting test items to measure the selected components, and selecting health-related standards to evaluate physical fitness.

A major criterion for the selection of test items and standards for the BPFT was validity. It was necessary to establish a framework for health-related physical fitness. Once this framework was determined, test items and standards were selected on the basis of logic, a review of literature, and data deemed relevant to validity. The theoretical conceptual basis for the test and other information regarding validity are discussed and summarized in chapter 2 to the extent necessary to appropriately interpret results of testing. More detailed information on validity is part of *The Fitness Challenge: Software for the Brockport Physical Fitness Test* (Short & Winnick, 1999).

A second criterion for selection of test items was reliability. All the test items recommended are believed to be reliable. Many data were found in the literature regarding the reliability of test items, and additional data supporting test-item reliability were collected as part of Project Target. These data are summarized in chapter 2. Again, readers may obtain more detailed information in *The Fitness Challenge: Software for the Brockport Physical Fitness Test* (Short & Winnick, 1999).

A third criterion for the selection of test items and standards was the extent to which test items could be used for different classes of youngsters. Preference was given to test items and standards that could be applied to youngsters with and without disabilities and that are found in appropriate tests of physical fitness designed for the general population. In particular, test items from the Prudential *FITNESSGRAM* were selected so that the BPFT could be easily coordinated by users of that test. Preference was also given to test items that could be administered to both males and females, to youngsters of various ages between 10 and 17, and to youngsters with various disabilities.

The fourth criterion of primary importance was to select test items that were believed to measure different physical fitness traits or abilities but that encompassed the components of physical fitness selected and defined for this test. This was done so that each item in the test adds new information about the ability of the youngster. Additional secondary criteria were also applied in the selection of test items. To the extent possible, items that are reasonably familiar to physical educators, economical in terms of time and expense, and that could be feasibly administered in field situations were selected.

TARGET POPULATIONS

The BPFT may be used with youngsters both with and without disabilities. It was developed for use with youngsters with disabilities, specifically those with visual impairments, mental retardation, and orthopedic impairments including cerebral palsy, spinal cord injuries, congenital anomalies, and amputations. However, a health-related, criterion-referenced test for people with disabilities builds on and closely relates to the physical fitness of youngsters in the general population. Definitions and classifications associated with these target groups are presented in the following sections.

General Population

Youngsters in the general population (GP) include those without disabilities. They are free from impairments or disabilities that influence test results.

Youngsters With Mental Retardation

In view of the continual change in terminology and definitions concerned with mental retardation (MR), it is necessary to clarify the meaning of mental retardation and its relationship to physical fitness for purposes of this test. The American Association on Mental Retardation (1992) offers the following definition:

> *Mental retardation refers to substantial limitations in present functioning. It is characterized by significantly subaverage intellectual functioning, existing concurrently with related limitations in two or more of the following applicable adaptive skill areas: communication, self-care, home living, social skills, community use, self-direction, health and safety, functional academics, leisure, and work. Mental retardation manifests before age 18.*

Although most youngsters with mental retardation have no limitations in physical fitness, others with mental retardation may exhibit limitations ranging from mild to severe. They may require slight to marked modifications in testing to measure physical fitness.

Youngsters with mental retardation and mild limitations in physical fitness include people requiring intermittent or limited support in learning or performing test items, who require substantial modifications to test items or alternative test items to measure one or more components of physical fitness. These individuals are capable of levels of fitness consistent with good health, can participate in games and leisure activities in selected appropriate environments, and can perform activities of daily living. Youngsters with mental retardation with mild limitations are perhaps best associated with the lower levels of mild mental retardation and the moderate mental retardation classifications associated with other systems.

Youngsters with mental retardation who have severe limitations generally have a need for extensive or pervasive support related to physical fitness. They require significant help in learning and performing physical fitness test items. They need alternative test items or marked modifications in measuring one or more components of physical fitness. Valid assessment of physical fitness of this group using typical health-related physical fitness tests may not be possible. Measurement of physical activity may be preferred for this group rather than assessment using physical fitness test items, which typically place an individual on an achievement scale. Task-analyzed test items may be suitable as test items of physical fitness for this group, and these individuals often require physical assistance as they perform these test items. Table 1.1 summarizes limitations and needs related to physical fitness testing of youngsters with mental retardation.

Table 1.1　Limitations and Needs of Youngsters With Mental Retardation for Physical Fitness Testing

Limitation	Needs
None	Have no unique physical fitness needs and require no unique modification or support in learning and performing physical fitness tests. The desired physical fitness profile and standards to evaluate physical fitness are identical to those for youngsters without disabilities.
Mild	Have mild limitations in physical fitness requiring intermittent or limited support in learning or performing test items; may require substantial modifications to test items or alternative test items to measure one or more components of physical fitness. Can demonstrate physical fitness on an achievement scale. Adjusted standards for assessing physical fitness may be appropriate. The desired physical fitness profile leans toward or closely relates to that of nondisabled youngsters.
Severe	Because of severe limitations, need extensive or pervasive support in learning and performing test items; need alternative test items or marked modifications in measuring one or more components of physical fitness. Valid assessment of physical fitness using test items designed to place individuals on an achievement scale may not be possible. May require assessment involving physical activity rather than physical fitness; will generally need individualized criterion-referenced standards for assessment of physical fitness.

Youngsters With Visual Impairment

Visual impairment (VI), including blindness (BL), is defined as an impairment in vision that, even with correction, adversely affects a child's educational performance. The term includes both partial sight and blindness. Categories of blindness given in table 1.2 are consistent with those used by the U.S. Association for Blind Athletes. The partial-sightedness category is an addition used with this test.

Table 1.2 Classification System for Youngsters With Visual Impairments

B1	Totally blind; those who may possess light perception but are unable to recognize hand shapes at any distance.
B2	Those perceiving hand shapes but with visual acuity of not better than 20/600 and/or those with less than 5° in the visual field.
B3	Those with visual acuity from 20/599 through 20/200 and/or those with 5° through 20° in visual field.
PS	Partially sighted; those with visual acuity from 20/199 through 20/70.

Youngsters With Spinal Cord Injury

For purposes of the BPFT, a spinal cord injury (SCI) is a condition that involves damage to the spinal cord resulting in motor and possibly sensory and muscular impairment. It includes traumatic as well as congenital spinal cord injury or malfunction. The level and extent of damage affect the nature and degree of impairment and disability. A complete spinal cord injury results in total loss of sensory, motor, and autonomic functions below the neurological level of spinal cord damage. An incomplete injury results in a partial but not total loss of function below the level of injury. The BPFT includes test items for individuals who have low-level quadriplegia or paraplegia and who primarily use wheelchairs for locomotion in their activities of daily living. These test items also can be used for ambulatory youngsters with spinal cord injury.

To select test items and standards appropriately for measurement and evaluation of physical fitness, the BPFT uses a three-category classification of spinal cord injury, summarized in table 1.3. The categories are low-level quadriplegia (LLQ), paraplegia—wheelchair (PW), and paraplegia—ambulatory (PA).

Table 1.3 Classification System for Youngsters With Spinal Cord Injury

Category	Description
Low-level quadriplegia (LLQ)	Individuals with complete or incomplete spinal cord damage that results in neurological impairment of all four extremities and the trunk and individuals with lower cervical (C6-C8) neurological involvement.
Paraplegia—wheelchair (PW)	Individuals with complete or incomplete spinal cord injury below the cervical area resulting in motor loss in the lower extremities (paraplegia) and the need to use a wheelchair for daily living activities.
Paraplegia—ambulatory (PA)	Individuals with complete or incomplete spinal cord injury resulting in motor loss in the lower extremities but who ambulate in daily activities without the use of wheelchair assistance.

Youngsters With Cerebral Palsy

The BPFT adopts the definition of cerebral palsy (CP) and the classification system of the Cerebral Palsy International Sport and Recreation Association (CP-ISRA, 1993):

> *Cerebral palsy is a brain lesion which is non-progressive and causes variable impairment of the coordination, tone and strength of muscle action with the resulting inability of the person to maintain normal postures and perform normal movements.*

In an effort to describe the degree of impairment as it influences performance in physical activity and sport, CP-ISRA has developed a classification system based on a functional evaluation that includes an assessment of the extent of control of the lower extremity, trunk, upper extremity, and hand. This classification system is summarized in table 1.4. C1 includes individuals with the most severe involvement (e.g., those who depend on an electric wheelchair or assistance for mobility), while C8, the highest class, includes those who are minimally affected (e.g., those who can run and jump freely). The first four classes are appropriate for those who use wheelchairs, and the second four are for those who are ambulatory.

Youngsters With Congenital Anomalies and Amputations

For the purposes of the BPFT, individuals with congenital anomalies include youngsters with fully or partially deformed extremities at birth. Individuals with amputations are those who are missing part or all of one or more of their extremities. Amputations may be congenital or acquired. The classification system, tests, and standards of the BPFT assume that these individuals are nondisabled except for their congenital anomalies and amputations (CA/A). Individuals who have physical conditions or diseases in addition to congenital anomalies and amputations must have programs more specifically personalized for them with medical consultation.

For the BPFT, individuals are subclassified according to limb involvement. The specific location of limb involvement is not typically a factor in subclassification.

Table 1.4   Classification System for Youngsters With Cerebral Palsy

Category	Description
C1	Individuals with severe spastic quadriplegia with or without athetosis or with poor functional range of movement and poor functional strength in all extremities and trunk; individuals with severe athetoid quadriplegia with or without spasticity with poor functional strength and control. In either case, individuals depend on electric wheelchair or assistance for mobility and are unable to functionally propel a manual wheelchair.
C2	Individuals with severe to moderate spastic quadriplegia with or without athetosis or with severe athetoid quadriplegia with fair function in the less-affected side. Poor functional strength in all extremities and trunk but able to propel a manual wheelchair. Further classifications are C2U if the individual exhibits relatively better upper-body abilities than lower-body abilities and C2L if the individual exhibits relatively greater lower-body than upper-body abilities.
C3	Individuals with moderate quadriplegia or severe hemiplegia resulting in use of a wheelchair for activities of daily living who can propel a manual wheelchair independently and have almost full functional strength in the dominant upper extremity.
C4	Individuals with moderate to severe diplegia with good functional strength and minimal limitation or control problems in the upper limbs or trunk. A wheelchair is usually chosen for sport.
C5	Individuals with moderate diplegia or triplegia who may require the use of assistive devices in walking but not necessarily when standing or throwing. Problems with dynamic balance are possible.
C6	Individuals with moderate athetosis or ataxia who ambulate without aids. Athetosis is the most prevalent factor, although some with spastic quadriplegia (i.e., more arm involvement than in ambulant diplegia) may fit this class. All four limbs usually show functional involvement in sports movements. Individuals in the C6 class usually have more control problems in upper limbs than those in C5 but usually have better function in lower limbs, particularly when running.
C7	Individuals with ambulant hemiplegia and spasticity on one side of the body who ambulate without assistive devices but often with a limp due to spasticity in a lower limb. Good functional ability on dominant side of body.
C8	Individuals who are minimally affected by spastic diplegia, spastic hemiplegia, or monoplegia or who are minimally affected by athetosis or ataxia.

Adapted, by permission, from Cerebral Palsy International Sport and Recreation Association (CP-ISRA), 1993, *CP-ISRA Handbook, 5th ed.*, (Heteren, Netherlands: CP-ISRA).

2

The Conceptual Framework

The Brockport Physical Fitness Test is a criterion-referenced test of health-related fitness. In a criterion-referenced approach, test scores obtained by youngsters are compared with standards that are thought to be associated with some index of positive health. It is important that test users understand the bases for these standards when assessing a youngster's performance.

The framework for developing the BPFT is represented by figure 2.1. This schematic, which is modified from a model described by Bouchard and Shephard (1994), should be helpful in understanding how test items and standards were selected. Relationships among physical activity, health, and health-related physical fitness depicted in the paradigm are discussed in the following sections.

PHYSICAL ACTIVITY

Physical activity consists of any bodily movement produced by skeletal muscle resulting in a substantial increase over resting energy expenditure (Bouchard & Shephard, 1994). Although categories of physical activity can also include work and domestic chores (Shephard, 1994), the Brockport approach focuses on two categories: physical education and leisure-time activity. Subsets of these two categories are shown in the schematic: exercise, sport, training, dance, and play. These types of physical activity can be performed in different patterns as dictated by frequency, intensity, and duration variables. In the Brockport approach the primary role of physical activity is related to the conditioning benefit it provides in developing health-related physical fitness.

HEALTH

Health has been defined as a "human condition with physical, social, and psychological dimensions, each characterized on a continuum with positive and

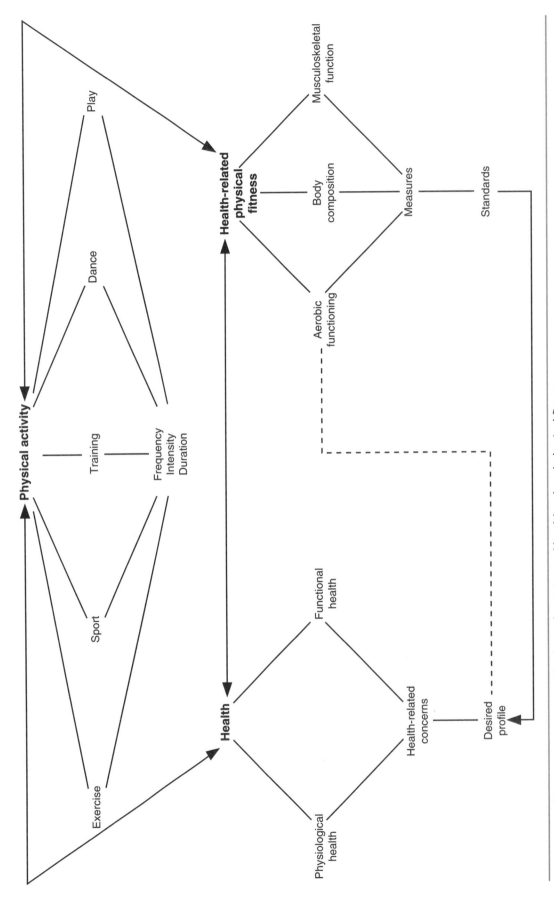

Figure 2.1 Relationship among health, physical activity, and health-related physical fitness.

negative poles. Positive health is associated with a capacity to enjoy life and to withstand challenges; it is not merely the absence of disease. Negative health is associated with morbidity and, in the extreme, with premature mortality" (Bouchard & Shephard, 1994 p. 84). In the Brockport paradigm, health is conceived as consisting of two general constructs: physiological health and functional health. Physiological health is related to the organic well-being of the individual. Indices of physiological health include traits or capacities that are associated with well-being, absence of a disease or condition, or low risk of developing a disease or a condition. Appropriate levels of body composition and aerobic capacity are examples of indices of good physiological health. Functional health is related to the physical capability of the individual. Indices of functional health include the ability to perform important tasks independently and the ability to independently sustain the performance of those tasks. Ability to perform activities of daily living (ADLs), ability to sustain physical activity, and ability to participate in leisure activities are examples of indices of good functional health. Both physiological health and functional health contribute to a person's capacity to enjoy life and to withstand challenges; both provide indices of health that serve as bases for health-related physical fitness standards.

HEALTH-RELATED PHYSICAL FITNESS

The Brockport definition of health-related physical fitness is as follows:

> *Health-related fitness refers to those components of fitness that are affected by habitual physical activity and relate to health status. It is defined as a state characterized by (a) an ability to perform and sustain daily activities and (b) demonstration of traits or capacities that are associated with a low risk of premature development of diseases and conditions related to movement (adapted from Pate, 1988).*

The health-related components of fitness adopted for this test include aerobic functioning, body composition, and musculoskeletal functioning. Aerobic functioning encompasses both aerobic capacity (maximal oxygen uptake, or $\dot{V}O_2$max) and aerobic behavior (the ability to perform aerobic activity at specified levels of intensity and duration). Body composition provides an indication of the degree of leanness or fatness of the body (usually percentage body fat). Musculoskeletal functioning is a component that combines measures of muscular strength, muscular endurance, and flexibility or range of motion. The relationship of these elements is evident when combining them, especially when designing a fitness program. Improving the range of motion of a joint in a youngster with a disability, for instance, may require improving the extensibility of the agonistic muscle while improving the strength of the antagonistic muscle.

A PERSONALIZED APPROACH

Field-based, norm-referenced or criterion-referenced tests of physical fitness that have been developed and used with youngsters in the past few years exhibit several identifiable characteristics. Important here is the fact that they have been developed largely on an assumed commonality of factors such as physical fitness purposes, needs, test items, and standards. Individualization within tests typically has been limited to and has focused on age and sex considerations. Thus tests typically have consisted of a standard number of items that are performed in a specific way and are evaluated using a general-population standard. Also, tests have usually been developed *for* youngsters rather than *with* youngsters.

Although such tests clearly have value for the hypothetical typical youngster, they also clearly have limited value for youngsters with disabilities. The health-related concerns of youngsters with disabilities exceed, as well as differ from, those of youngsters in the general population. Specific disabilities may affect movement modes, movement abilities, and health-related physical fitness potential. For example, an individual completely paralyzed in the lower extremities who uses a wheelchair is unable to demonstrate aerobic functioning by running a mile. A different way of demonstrating and assessing aerobic functioning is necessary for such an individual. An individual with double leg amputation at or near the hip joint requires different maximal oxygen intake and body mass index standards to validly evaluate fitness from those for nondisabled peers. Clearly, test items to measure physical fitness should be different for youngsters with such disabilities in some instances. At times, health-related concerns and subcomponents of physical fitness need to be different from those selected for nondisabled peers. Because of the wide variation in the needs and abilities of youngsters with disabilities, the specific nature of a physical fitness test should be developed through personal association and interaction with the youngsters being tested to the extent possible. When such interaction occurs, the test becomes personalized as well as individualized. Personalization and individualization have not traditionally played an important role in the development of physical fitness tests.

Because of such problems with traditional fitness tests, the BPFT has incorporated a personalized approach to physical fitness testing and assessment. After the development of a health-related, criterion-referenced physical fitness orientation and a corresponding definition of physical fitness, the following steps are suggested for personalizing a health-related, criterion-referenced physical fitness test:

- Identify and select health-related concerns of importance to the youngster.
- Establish a desired personalized fitness profile with (or for, as necessary) the youngster.
- Select components and subcomponents of physical fitness to be assessed.
- Select test items to measure selected fitness components and subcomponents.
- Select health-related, criterion-referenced standards to evaluate physical fitness.

Each of these steps is discussed in the sections that follow.

Health-Related Concerns

After acceptance of a health-related physical fitness orientation, the first step in developing a personalized physical fitness test for a person or class of people is to identify and select health-related concerns that the test will address or emphasize. In practice, health concerns of the general population are reviewed to determine whether they are appropriate for individuals with disabilities. These health concerns provide bases for standards in which health status is the criterion. For example, the developers of Prudential *FITNESSGRAM* identified the following health-related concerns to be addressed by their test: high blood pressure, coronary heart disease, obesity, diabetes, some forms of cancer, lower-back flexibility, functional health, and other health problems. These may also be the basic concerns of individuals with disabilities. However, individuals with disabilities may also have additional health-related concerns. For example, a youngster with a spinal cord injury requiring a wheelchair for ambulation may have health-related concerns typical of nondisabled youngsters but may have additional concerns such as the ability to sustain aerobic activity; range of motion or flexibility of the hips or upper body; and strength and endurance to lift and transfer the body independently, lift the body to prevent decubitus ulcers (pressure sores), or propel a wheelchair manually. Health-related concerns such as these may be drawn from professional literature, expert opinion, opinions of parents and youngsters themselves, or other sources deemed appropriate. The key is to identify and select health-related concerns most relevant and important to the individual.

Desired Personalized Profile

Once health-related concerns are identified, a desired, personalized physical fitness profile is developed for a person or class of people. A desired profile establishes the direction or broad goal(s) for a health-related physical fitness program. A profile statement can be written that implicitly or explicitly identifies the components of physical fitness that will be addressed and that expresses the underlying value of the component to the health-related concerns. The profile thus serves as a reference for a desired personal state of physical fitness. If appropriate, the profile serves as a basis for the selection of test items and standards for evaluating health-related physical fitness. Desired profiles should reflect at least minimal acceptable levels of physical fitness. However, they may also reflect preferred levels. A possible desired physical fitness profile for nondisabled youngsters could be described as follows:

All individuals should possess, at minimum, levels of aerobic capacity and body composition consistent with positive health, adequate flexibility for functional health (especially good functioning of the lower and upper back), and levels of abdominal, trunk extensor, and upper-body strength and endurance adequate for independent living and participation in physical activities.

Analysis of the health-related concerns and needs of an individual with a spinal cord injury suggests an alternative profile, such as this possibility:

Individuals with spinal cord injury should possess, at minimum, levels of aerobic behavior and body composition consistent with positive health; adequate levels of flexibility and range of motion to perform activities of daily living and inhibit contractures; adequate levels of muscular strength and endurance for wheelchair users to lift and transfer the body and propel a wheelchair; muscular strength and endurance to counteract muscular weakness; and fitness levels needed to enhance the performance of daily living activities (including sport activities).

Analysis of these two profiles reveals both similarities and dissimilarities. Both profiles reflect a desire for appropriate levels of aerobic functioning. However, the profile for the individual with spinal cord injury focuses on a desired level of aerobic behavior consistent with positive health, whereas the profile for the nondisabled individual focuses on appropriate levels of aerobic capacity. The two profiles are identical in regard to desired levels of body composition. Both profiles identify the importance of musculoskeletal functioning for independent living and participation in physical activities, but they differ in addressing the specific musculoskeletal needs of the individuals.

Components of Physical Fitness

Components of physical fitness associated with the BPFT include aerobic functioning, body composition, and musculoskeletal functioning. Each of these include specific subcomponents that can be selected for a personalized physical fitness test. For example, within aerobic functioning, aerobic capacity or aerobic behavior, or both can be selected for a personalized physical fitness test. Subcomponents of body composition include percentage body fat and the ratio of weight to height. Musculoskeletal functioning includes subcomponents of muscular strength, muscular endurance, and range of motion or flexibility. Components and more specific subcomponents to be included in a personalized test should be consistent with the desired personalized profile. The BPFT recommends that all three components of physical fitness be included in every personalized test of physical fitness to the extent possible.

Test Items, Validity, and Reliability

Once components and subcomponents of health-related physical fitness are selected in consideration of health-related concerns, test items are selected to measure the components. Validity, reliability, the extent of use for different classes of youngsters, the extent of information provided by a test item, economy of time and expense, user friendliness, and feasibility in field situations are among the criteria for the selection of test items.

A total of 27 test items are included in the BPFT. Selection guides are provided in chapter 4 to help testers select those tests that are most appropriate for a youngster with a particular disability. Each test item is listed in table 2.1 along with its associated component or subcomponent of fitness, target populations, and a summary of available validity and reliability information. References are provided where appropriate. Readers are referred to the technical manual of *The Fitness Challenge: Software for the Brockport Physical Fitness Test* (Short & Winnick, 1999) for more detailed information on validity and reliability as well as background on the selection and attainability of standards. Readers may also wish to consult the Project Target final report (Winnick & Short, 1998) for information on validity and reliability.

Essentially three different types of validity are claimed for the various test items: concurrent, construct, and logical (or content). When an item has concurrent validity, it has a relationship with some criterion measure of the component or subcomponent of fitness being measured (e.g., $\dot{V}O_2$max, percentage body fat). Evidence of concurrent validity is provided for the 20-m PACER, 16-m PACER, one-mile run/walk, skinfolds, body mass index (BMI), and dumbbell press. In most cases correlations with the criterion measure could be considered to be at least moderate (r = .70-.89).

Table 2.1 Summary of Test-Item Validity and Reliability

Test item	Fitness component/subcomponent	Target population	Validity	Reliability
PACER (20 m)	Aerobic capacity	GP, MR, BL, CA/A	High content; moderate concurrent (Cureton, 1994a)	$r = .89$ (GP) (Leger, Mercier, Gadoury, & Lambert, 1988) $\alpha = .97$ (MR) (Short & Winnick, 1999)
PACER (16 m)	Aerobic capacity	MR	$r = .77$ with peak $\dot{V}O_2$ (MR) (Fernhall, Pitetti, Vukavich, Stubbs, Hansen, Winnick & Short, 1996)	$\alpha = .96-.98$ (MR) (Short & Winnick, 1999)
One-mile run/walk	Aerobic capacity	GP, BL, CA/A	$r = .60-.85$ with $\dot{V}O_2$max (Cureton, 1994a)	Usually highly reliable for adolescents (Safrit & Wood, 1995)
Target aerobic movement test (TAMT)	Aerobic behavior	MR, CP, SCI, CA/A	Logical	$P = .92$ (SCI) (Rimmer, Connor-Kuntz, Winnick, & Short, 1997)
Skinfolds	Body composition	All	$r = .88-.89$ with % body fat (Lohman, 1994)	Interrater reliability is high (> .95) (Safrit & Wood, 1995)
Body mass index (BMI)	Body composition	GP, MR, BL, CP	$r = .70-.82$ with % body fat (Lohman, 1992)	Very high (Lohman, 1994)
Reverse curl	Upper-body strength/endurance	SCI	Logical	No data available
Seated push-up	Upper-body strength/endurance	CP, SCI, CA/A	Logical	No data available
40-m push/walk	General strength/endurance	CP	Logical	No data available
Wheelchair ramp test	Upper-body strength/endurance	CP	Logical	No data available
Push-up	Upper-body strength/endurance	GP, BL	Logical (Plowman & Corbin, 1994)	Generally reliable (.60–.96) (Plowman & Corbin, 1994)

(continued)

Table 2.1 *(continued)*

Test item	Fitness component/ subcomponent	Target population	Validity	Reliability
Pull-up	Upper-body strength/ endurance	GP, BL, CA/A	Logical (Plowman & Corbin, 1994); construct (Winnick & Short, 1982)	Generally reliable (.79–.91) (Plowman & Corbin, 1994)
Modified pull-up	Upper-body strength/ endurance	GP, BL	Logical (Plowman & Corbin, 1994)	Generally reliable (.56–.91) (Plowman & Corbin, 1994)
Dumbbell press	Upper-body strength/ endurance	CP, SCI, CA/A	Logical; $r = .81$ (GP) with bench press (Short & Winnick, 1999)	$\alpha = .98$ (MR) (Short & Winnick, 1999)
Bench press	Upper-body strength/ endurance	MR, SCI, CA/A	Logical	$\alpha = .91$ (MR); $\alpha = .92$ (GP) (Short & Winnick, 1999)
Grip strength	Upper-body strength/ endurance	MR, CP, SCI, CA/A	Construct (Winnick & Short, 1982); logical	Most coefficients in the .90s (Safrit & Wood, 1995)
Isometric push-up	Upper-body strength/ endurance	MR	Logical	$R = .83$ (Eichstaedt & Lavay, 1992) $\alpha = .83$ (MR) (Short & Winnick, 1999)
Extended arm hang	Upper-body strength/ endurance	MR	Logical	$\alpha = .85$ (MR) (Short & Winnick, 1999)
Flexed arm hang	Upper-body strength/ endurance	GP, MR, BL, CA/A	Construct (Winnick & Short, 1982); logical (Plowman & Corbin, 1994)	$\alpha = .84$–.96 (Daquila, 1982) $\alpha = .93$ (MR) (Short & Winnick, 1999)
Trunk lift	Trunk/abdominal function	GP, MR, BL, CA/A	Logical (Plowman & Corbin, 1994)	$P = .89$ (MR) (Short & Winnick, 1999)
Curl-up	Trunk/abdominal function	GP, BL, CA/A	Logical (Plowman & Corbin, 1994)	$R = .93$–.97 (Robertson & Magnusdottir, 1987)
Modified curl-up	Trunk/abdominal function	MR	Logical (Jette, Sidney, & Cicutti, 1984)	$r = .88$ (Jette et al., 1984) $\alpha = .82$ (Short & Winnick, 1999)
Target stretch test (TST)	Flexibility/ROM	CP, SCI, CA/A	Logical; $P = .85$ with goniometry-based scoring (Short & Winnick, 1999)	$\alpha = .92$ for interrater reliability for similar protocol (Short & Winnick, 1999)

Table 2.1

Test item	Fitness component/ subcomponent	Target population	Validity	Reliability
Shoulder stretch	Flexibility/ROM	CP, MR, BL, CA/A	Logical	α = .83–.94 (MR) (Short & Winnick, 1999)
Modified Apley test	Flexibility/ROM	CP, SCI, CA/A	Logical	No data available
Modified Thomas test	Flexibility/ROM	CP, SCI, CA/A	Logical	No data available
Back-saver sit & reach	Flexibility/ROM	GP, MR, BL, CA/A	Logical (Plowman & Corbin, 1994)	α = .95–.97 (GP) (Patterson, Wiksten, Ray, Flanders, & Sanphy, 1996) α = .95–.96 (MR) (Short & Winnick, 1999)

ROM = range of motion CP = cerebral palsy R = intraclass reliability coefficent
GP = general population SCI = spinal cord injury α = Cronbach's alpha coefficient
MR = mental retardation CA/A = congenital anomaly/amputation P = proportion of agreement
BL = blindness r = interclass reliability coefficient

Construct validity may be claimed when a test item "loads" with related items in a factor analysis; these related items statistically and logically define a *construct* (e.g., strength, body composition), and each item that defines a construct can be used to measure it. Construct validity is used to support, at least in part, the pull-up, dominant grip strength, and flexed arm hang. Earlier factor-analytic work by Winnick and Short (1982) established that dominant grip strength is a test that can help define a factor that comprises items requiring strength applied over short time intervals. Pull-ups and flexed arm hangs typically loaded on a different factor, one that appeared to have a greater endurance component. All three items, therefore, seem to appropriately measure upper-body strength and endurance (where *upper body* has been determined logically).

Logical validity is claimed for most items in the BPFT battery. In each case a rationale exists for relating a test item to some important criterion. Sometimes the rationale is anatomical (e.g., the curl-up test measures the strength and endurance of the abdominal muscles; the modified Thomas test measures the length of the hip flexors; the back-saver sit and reach assesses the flexibility of the hamstrings), and other times it is functional (e.g., the wheelchair ramp test evaluates the ability to negotiate a one-step standard incline; the 40-m push/walk tests the ability to achieve functional speed for mobility about the community), but in each case the test purports to measure an aspect of fitness with health-related implications. Although the technical manual of *The Fitness Challenge: Software for the Brockport Physical Fitness Test* (Short & Winnick, 1999) is the best place to find more information on logical validity, the section "The Bases for Standards" later in this chapter provides some additional material that should be helpful. Whether established statistically or logically, evidence of validity is provided for each item in the BPFT.

A variety of statistics are used to demonstrate reliability on a test-retest basis. The interclass r (the Pearson product-moment coefficient), the intraclass R, and Cronbach's alpha (α) all have been used to estimate the reliability of the test items in the BPFT. The intraclass R and Cronbach's alpha are preferred measures of reliability because they account for more sources of measurement error than does the interclass r. Proportion of agreement (P) is a reliability estimate of a criterion-referenced test and provides information on the consistency of pass/fail decisions over two administrations of the test. Generally, reliability coefficients greater than .70 are considered minimally acceptable estimates of score consistency. Values in the .90 range usually are considered to indicate a high degree of reliability. Test-retest reliability coefficients associated with BPFT items generally reflect at least minimal levels of acceptability, and several indicate items that are highly reliable. Statistics on reliability are unavailable for six items in the battery. Scoring for those items seems to be fairly objective, which should help control that source of measurement error. Again, readers are referred to the technical manual of *The Fitness Challenge: Software for the Brockport Physical Fitness Test* (Short & Winnick, 1999) for more information on test-item reliability.

Standards for Evaluating Physical Fitness

Once test items have been selected to measure components and subcomponents of physical fitness, standards are selected to serve as a basis for evaluating fitness from a health-status orientation. Standards selected to assess physical fitness can reflect minimal or preferred levels of fitness. Interpretations of physical fitness status should be made by evaluating implicit or explicit standards reflected in the desired profile, which in turn reflect a desired level of health-related physical fitness.

PROFILES, TEST ITEMS, AND STANDARDS WITHIN COMPONENTS OF PHYSICAL FITNESS

Personalization implies that testers, once they identify appropriate health-related concerns, can write their own physical fitness profiles (in consultation with youngsters where appropriate), select their own test items related to components of health-related fitness, and decide on their own standards. The BPFT provides information on profiles, items, and standards, which testers can adopt for use with youngsters as appropriate.

The BPFT provides 10 profile statements related to three components of health-related fitness: aerobic functioning, body composition, and musculoskeletal functioning (see figures 2.2-2.6). Two profile statements each are given for aerobic functioning and body composition and six for musculoskeletal functioning (four related primarily to strength and endurance and two to flexibility or range of motion). Test items and standards are recommended for each of the 10 profile statements with the target populations in mind. Testers can select profiles, tests, and standards from the options provided. Testers always have the additional option to adjust or substitute material.

Figures 2.2 through 2.6 at the end of this chapter show relationships among fitness components and subcomponents, the 10 profile statements, test items, and standards. Standards are either general or specific. A general standard is one that is associated with the general population. It is a test score that is related to either functional or physiological health and is attainable by youngsters whose performance is not significantly limited by impairment. A specific standard also reflects functional or physiological health, but it has been adjusted in some way to account for the effects of a specific impairment on performance. General standards may be recommended for the general population and youngsters with certain disabilities. Specific standards are provided only for selected test items for specific target populations.

When a standard is general, testers usually have two levels from which to choose: minimal and preferred. A minimal general standard is considered an acceptable score. It meets the lowest acceptable general criterion of health associated with a particular test. Most youngsters should be able to attain the appropriate minimal standard provided. A preferred general standard is meant to convey a higher level of fitness and is therefore more desirable. A preferred general standard represents a good level of fitness and is one that most youngsters find challenging. In a few instances, a single general standard rather than minimal or preferred general standards is recommended and provided. In such instances, the single standard is associated with a good and preferred level of fitness.

If a standard either is not available for a particular test item or is believed to be inappropriate for a specific youngster, testers are encouraged to develop individualized standards by which to assess performance. An individualized standard is a desired level of attainment for an individual in an area of health status, established in consideration of the individual's present level of performance and expectation for progress. It is not necessarily a health-related standard. For a standard to be health-related it must meet an established general or specific level reflecting health.

THE BASES FOR STANDARDS

There are 27 test items in the BPFT, categorized under three components of health-related fitness. The large number of test items provides testers with greater flexibility when personalizing the test. In most cases, testers select between four and six test items to be used with a particular youngster.

Each of the test items, categorized by fitness component, are identified in the following sections. A brief discussion of the bases for criterion-referenced standards associated with each item is also provided. Testers need to understand the bases for the standards to interpret results of testing.

Aerobic Functioning

Aerobic functioning refers to that component of physical fitness that permits an individual to sustain large-muscle, dynamic, moderate- to high-intensity activity for prolonged periods of time. This component depends primarily on the efficiency or development of heart, lung, blood, and skeletal muscle metabolic functions of the body. Aerobic functioning is perhaps the most important of the health-related components of fitness because it is clearly related to both functional and physiological aspects of health. Possessing an adequate level of aerobic functioning allows a person to sustain physical activity for work, play, and emergencies and may reduce risk of developing certain diseases. In the BPFT, aerobic functioning has two separate but related subcomponents: aerobic capacity and aerobic behavior.

Aerobic capacity refers to the highest rate of oxygen that can be consumed by a person while exercising. The more fit a person is, the greater his or her aerobic capacity. In addition to enhancing performance in endurance activities, acceptable levels of aerobic capacity are associated with a reduced risk of developing certain diseases and conditions in adulthood, including high blood pressure, coronary heart disease, obesity, diabetes, and some forms of cancer (Blair, Kohl, Paffenbarger, Clark, Cooper & Gibbons, 1989; Blair, Kohl, Gordon, & Paffenbarger, 1992).

A laboratory measurement of maximal oxygen uptake ($\dot{V}O_2$max) is generally considered to be the best measure of aerobic capacity, but aerobic capacity also can be estimated in a field setting. The PACER (16 m and 20 m) and the one-mile run/walk are test items used to estimate aerobic capacity in the BPFT. Minimal general standards for each of these items are based on a minimal level of $\dot{V}O_2$max believed to be consistent with positive health and functional capacity for daily living in adult men and women. These $\dot{V}O_2$max values have been adjusted for age to account for developmental factors (Cureton & Warren, 1990). Preferred standards are based on a level of $\dot{V}O_2$max that is thought to be good and is associated with lower disease risk and mortality in adults (Cureton, 1994a and 1994b). It is believed that some additional health and functional capacity benefits can be attained by meeting the preferred standards.

In the BPFT the aerobic capacity general standards (both minimal and preferred) are sometimes adjusted to reflect disability-specific concerns. For instance, youngsters who are blind may need to participate in running items with some form of tactual assistance or guidance (e.g., guide wire, sighted partner). Such an encumbrance requires more energy than running unassisted. Consequently, minimal aerobic capacity standards are somewhat lower for runners who require tactual assistance to account for the higher energy demands of their activity. For those who run with assistance, the specific standards are consistent with the recommendation made by Buell (1983), which called for a 10-percentile adjustment in assessment using norm-referenced standards. Assisted blind runners who attain general standards likely possess levels of aerobic capacity greater than those possessed by youngsters in the general population because running inefficiency is believed to influence performance. Youngsters who are mentally retarded also may require an adjustment to $\dot{V}O_2$max standards. In the BPFT the minimal specific standards are 10% lower than those for the general population, in accordance with the consistent performance discrepancy on measurements of aerobic capacity observed between youngsters with and without mental retardation. Shephard (1990) estimates that the scores of individuals with mental retardation are 8% to 12% below those of nondisabled peers of the same age.

In some cases it is not yet possible to estimate aerobic capacity accurately in a field setting. Such an estimate is particularly problematic for those with physical disabilities, especially cerebral palsy. The extent and nature of the impairment, type of wheelchair or other assistive device that may be used, and type of surface on which the test is conducted all contribute to the complexity of the estimate. There is also a belief, which we share, that functional health-related needs represented by aerobic behavior are relevant and important to the individual and can be more accurately and feasibly measured in field-based tests for people with disabilities than can aerobic capacity. For these reasons a measure of aerobic capacity is not recommended for certain youngsters with disabilities. Instead, a measure of aerobic behavior is suggested.

Aerobic behavior refers to the ability to sustain physical activity of a specific intensity for a particular duration. The measure of aerobic behavior associated with the BPFT is the Target Aerobic Movement Test (TAMT). Individuals who demonstrate the ability to sustain moderate physical activity for 15 min meet the general minimal standard for health-related aerobic behavior. An exercise heart rate of at least 70% of maximal predicted heart rate, adjusted for disability or mode of exercise, represents moderate exercise. The TAMT actually has two standards: one for intensity and one for duration.

The ability to sustain at least moderate-level activity for 15 min has positive implications for functional health, especially for ADLs and participation in leisure-time pursuits (including games and sports). Furthermore, this level of activity is believed to reflect behavior that, when performed regularly, is consistent with existing general recommendations for health enhancement or maintenance (American College of Sports Medicine, 1990, 1995; U.S. Department of Health and Human Services, 1996) and is sufficiently intense to stimulate an aerobic training effect (McArdle, Katch, & Katch, 1994).

The TAMT is an appropriate test for many youngsters both with and without disabilities. Adjustments to intensity requirements, however, are necessary under certain circumstances. If a youngster uses an arms-only form of exercise (e.g., propelling a wheelchair, cranking an arm ergometer, punching a speed bag) to elevate the heart rate, intensity standards are reduced to account for the fact that maximal predicted heart rate is lower for these forms of exercise (Shephard, 1990). Intensity standards also are adjusted for youngsters who have a spinal cord injury in the low cervical region (C6-C8). These adjustments attempt to account for different ways that quadriplegia affects heart rate and provide reasonable expectations for exercise intensity. These adjustments were developed by the Project Target Advisory Committee.

Body Composition

Body composition is the component of health-related physical fitness that pertains to the degree of leanness or fatness of the body. Body composition has implications for both functional health and physiological health. When fat levels in the body are too high, ability to lift or move the body is negatively affected. Similarly, obesity has been found to be associated with an increased risk of diabetes, coronary heart disease, high blood pressure, arthritis, various forms of cancer, and all-cause mortality (U.S. Department of Health and Human Services, 1996). Several studies have shown that skinfold thicknesses are related to higher levels of blood lipids, lipoproteins, blood pressure, and glucose tolerance in children (Lohman, 1994). Paffenbarger and Lee (1996) identified several studies indicating that obesity is a risk factor in the development of coronary heart disease.

Indicators of body composition in the BPFT are skinfolds and body mass index. Minimal general standards for body fat range from 10% to 25% body fat for males and from 17% to 32% for females. These percentages reflect minimally acceptable zones of percentage body fat. Research indicates that when percentage body fat exceeds the upper values in these ranges, there is an increase in mortality rates from cardiovascular disease (Lohman, 1994). Lower values are meant to convey that a youngster's health also may be negatively affected by low levels of body fatness (Lohman, 1994). The preferred general standards retain the lower percentage body fat values but reduce the upper values. Preferred general standards therefore range from 10% to 20% body fat for males and from 17% to 25% for females. These ranges are considered to be optimal for children and adolescents because there is a tendency for youngsters to get fatter with age (Lohman, 1994). It is recommended that skinfold measurements be taken only over areas with active muscles. No disability-specific standards are recommended for body composition. Regardless of disability, all youngsters need to maintain an appropriate level of body fat for health reasons.

Body mass index (BMI) is a second but less preferred measure of body composition. It is an indication of the appropriateness of a youngster's weight for his or her height. Weight and height values are used for computation of BMI. To enhance the evaluation of body composition using BMI, BMI values corresponding to various levels of percentage body fat using methods presented by Lohman (1994) have been developed and are presented in tables 4.10 and 4.11 within this manual. BMI can be matched to corresponding acceptable or minimal levels of percentage body fat, and thus the same standards can be used for purposes of evaluation. Testers should take extreme care to use accurate information for interpreting BMI scores for youngsters with physical disabilities. Underestimates of either height (e.g., due to contractures at the knees or hips) or weight (e.g., due to a missing limb or loss of active muscle mass) can invalidate the standards.

Musculoskeletal Functioning

Musculoskeletal functioning combines three traditional components of physical fitness: muscular strength, muscular endurance, and flexibility or range of motion. The relationship between musculoskeletal functioning and health (especially functional health) has a logical basis. Certain levels of strength, endurance, and flexibility are necessary to maintain good posture, live independently, and participate in leisure-time activities.

The bench press, dumbbell press, extended arm hang, flexed arm hang, dominant grip strength, isometric push-up, push-up, modified pull-up, pull-up, curl-up, modified curl-up, and trunk lift are all measures of musculoskeletal function, primarily muscular strength and endurance. Although each of these test items can be justified on the basis of logical validity, no specific level of strength and endurance has been identified as critical for health. Instead, criterion-referenced standards associated with these items are based primarily on expert opinion (Plowman & Corbin, 1994). The basis for the minimal general standards associated with some of these tests is to score at or above the 20th percentile for the general population. Preferred general standards are associated with the ability to score at or above the 60th percentile for the general population. For the trunk lift, a single general standard based on expert opinion and representing a good (preferred) level of fitness is used.

Specific standards for some of these muscular strength and endurance items are provided for youngsters with mental retardation and mild limitations in fitness. The literature consistently documents a performance discrepancy between youngsters who are mentally retarded and not mentally retarded on many measures of muscular strength and endurance. Factors such as motivation, fewer opportunities to train, fewer opportunities to participate in physical activity, poor instruction, and physiological factors have been cited by researchers attempting to explain the performance gap. Where specific standards are provided in the BPFT for youngsters who are mentally retarded, they are lower than the minimal general standards by a range of 25% to 50%. The particular percentage used is an estimate of the performance discrepancy identified for a specific item in previous research.

No specific standards are provided for youngsters with physical disabilities on these measures of muscular strength and endurance. Selecting appropriate test items is especially important for these youngsters. Youngsters with some form of paraplegia (due to either cerebral palsy or spinal cord injury) should be able to achieve general standards for upper-body measures involving the hands or arms but may have difficulty with measures involving the trunk or abdomen. Unilateral test items such as dominant grip strength and dumbbell press have the most relevance for youngsters with some types of cerebral palsy, particularly hemiplegia, and for single-limb amputees.

The reverse curl, seated push-up, and 40-m push/walk also assess muscular strength and endurance and are most appropriate for youngsters with certain types of physical disabilities. Bases for specific standards for these items come from their relationship to ADLs. The specific standard for the reverse curl is tied directly to the functional ability of lifting a 1-lb (0.5-kg) weight one time. It is assumed that such an ability has functional significance for youngsters who are more severely disabled (especially those with low-level cervical spinal cord injury) who might hope to lift a lightweight object in performing ADLs.

The specific standard for the seated push-up is selected on the basis of two possibilities. The 5-s standard is related to the recommendation that wheelchair-users relieve the skin pressure on their buttocks and legs for approximately 5 s every 15 min. Such a regimen is believed to reduce risk of developing decubitus ulcers (Kosiak & Kottke, 1990). The 20-s specific standard for the seated push-up would be selected if health-related concerns relating to other ADL's (e.g., transferring) require longer strength or endurance needs.

The basis for the specific standard for the 40-m push/walk is potential for functional mobility. The minimal value for functional walking speed in adults is approximately 40 m/min (Waters, 1992). This value has been adopted as the specific standard, provided that it can be attained at a heart rate of 125 beats/min or less (see adjustments for disability in the description of this test item in chapter 5). If youngsters can travel at 40 m/min at this light intensity, it is assumed that they can maintain that functional speed over longer distances required for the performance of ADLs in the community.

The standards for the wheelchair ramp test are related to the American National Standards Institute (ANSI) recommendations that ramps be constructed with an incline ratio of 12 in. of run for every inch of rise in elevation. A ramp built to negotiate a 2-ft elevation, therefore, must be 24 ft long. For the ramp test, two possibilities for specific standards also exist. The first, a standard of 8 ft of run is linked to the ability to ascend 8 in. of elevation, or the height of approximately one step. Curb-cuts have a maximum rise of 8 in. and steps for stairs have a uniform height of 7 in. The second, the 15-ft standard, is actually a floating standard that can be matched to the length of a ramp (up to 30 ft) the youngster may encounter on a daily basis. Testers may set this standard anywhere between 15 and 30 ft, therefore, depending upon the mobility demands placed on the youngster on a daily basis.

The shoulder stretch, modified Apley test, modified Thomas test, back-saver sit and reach, and target stretch test (TST) are tests of flexibility or range of motion. The shoulder stretch and modified Apley test are tests of shoulder flexibility. The shoulder stretch is scored pass/fail and is justified solely on a logical basis. A passing score is a single general standard and indicates optimal shoulder flexibility. Only pass or fail standards are provided for the shoulder stretch.

The modified Apley test is scored on a scale of 0 to 3: 3 indicates optimal shoulder flexibility; 2 suggests enough shoulder flexibility to potentially perform functional activities such as washing, combing the hair, or removing a cap; 1 indicates the potential to perform functional activities such as eating and brushing the teeth; and 0 means insufficient flexibility to accomplish any of the tasks listed. A score of 3 is the general standard, and it is expected that most youngsters can achieve it. Specific standards are provided only for youngsters with more severe forms of cerebral palsy (classes C1 and C2).

The modified Thomas test measures hip flexibility but is recommended only for ambulatory youngsters. For the modified Thomas test, scores are tied to extent of limitation in the hip flexors: a score of 3 indicates optimal hip extension, 2 suggests some tightness in the hip flexors that results in an approximately 15° or smaller loss in range of motion, 1 means that the loss of range of motion is between approximately 15° and 30°, and 0 means loss of range of motion exceeds approximately 30°. The general standard is 3. A specific standard is provided only for youngsters with a type of cerebral palsy that typically restricts hip flexibility (class C5 and C7 for the affected side).

The back-saver sit and reach has been shown to validly measure hamstring flexibility. Sit-and-reach tests have been included in health-related fitness test batteries for a number of years because of a presumed relationship to low-back pain. Although research evidence has yet to confirm this relationship, anatomical logic for it is strong. Only general standards are provided in this manual. As with many test items of muscular strength and endurance, the standards on the back-saver sit and reach is based on expert opinion (Plowman & Corbin, 1994).

The target stretch test (TST) is a subjective measure of movement extent that can be applied to a number of joint actions. Individualized standards (those developed by testers for youngsters' specific needs) are recommended for some youngsters. For most youngsters, however, the basis for the minimal general standard is to have functional range of motion on at least one side of the body. Functional range of motion is represented by a score of 1 on the test. The Project Target Advisory Committee considered this a clinically acceptable level of range of motion that is generally obtainable and meets minimal requirements for functional activity. The preferred general standard, represented by a score of 2, depicts optimal range of motion for a particular joint. Youngsters who are free of physical impairments should strive for the preferred general standard on the TST.

Sources of Standards

Standards recommended in the BPFT come from a variety of sources. Several criterion-referenced, health-related standards appropriate for the general population and sometimes recommended for youngsters with disabilities were developed by the Cooper Institute for Aerobics Research (1992, 1999).[a] These include standards for the following items: $\dot{V}O_2$max, one-mile run/walk, 20-m PACER, skinfolds, percentage body fat, body mass index, curl-up, trunk lift, push-up, pull-up, modified pull-up, flexed arm hang, back-saver sit and reach, and shoulder stretch.

Standards for $\dot{V}O_2$max and the one-mile run/walk appearing in the Prudential *FITNESSGRAM* were based on procedures used and results attained by Cureton and Warren (1990), and standards for the 20-m PACER were based on the work of Leger et al. (1988). Use of $\dot{V}O_2$max and the one-mile run/walk in Prudential *FITNESSGRAM* is described by Cureton (1994a).

Standards related to body composition used in the Prudential *FITNESSGRAM* were developed as described by Lohman (1994). Lohman (personal communication, May 1997) subsequently provided additional skinfold and body mass index values associated with the BPFT's minimal general standards and preferred general standards.

---

[a]Standards associated with the 1992 Prudential *FITNESSGRAM* and the 1999 *FITNESSGRAM* are identical (Cooper Institute for Aerobics Research, 1992 and 1999). *FITNESSGRAM* is a registered trademark of the Cooper Institute for Aerobics Research (CIAR).

Standards associated with several musculoskeletal test items in the Prudential *FITNESSGRAM* were based on expert opinion following a review of normative data from nondisabled youngsters (Plowman & Corbin, 1994). These test items include the push-up, pull-up, modified pull-up, flexed arm hang, trunk lift, curl-up, shoulder stretch, and back-saver sit and reach. Standards reflecting performance of the general population on items not associated with the Prudential *FITNESSGRAM* were developed on the basis of data collected on 913 youngsters from the Brockport (New York) Central School District. Minimal and preferred standards related to performance of the general population on the dumbbell press, bench press, extended arm hang, dominant grip strength, and isometric push-up were based in part on these data. General standards for the modified Apley, modified Thomas, target stretch, and target aerobic movement tests were based on expert opinion (Project Target Advisory Committee, 1997).

Specific standards were also based on expert opinion, related literature, and data from samples of youngsters with disabilities. Data collected as a part of Project Target were used to field-test the suitability, attainability, and reliability of, and the standards for, the bench press, extended arm hang, flexed arm hang, modified curl-up, dominant grip strength, isometric push-up, seated push-up, reverse curl, 40-m push/walk, modified Apley and Thomas tests, 16-m and 20-m PACER, and the one-mile run/walk. Data associated with Project UNIQUE (Winnick & Short, 1985) were also consulted in selecting standards for the flexed arm hang, dominant grip strength, and skinfold measures. Recommended specific standards for youngsters with mental retardation were developed consulting data provided by Eichstaedt, Polacek, Wang, and Dohrman (1991); Hayden (1964); and the Canada Fitness Award (Government of Canada, Fitness and Amateur Sport, 1985). Standards associated with the TST are based on optimal levels of range of motion presented by Cole and Tobis (1990), and functional standards were recommended by the Project Target Advisory Committee (1997).

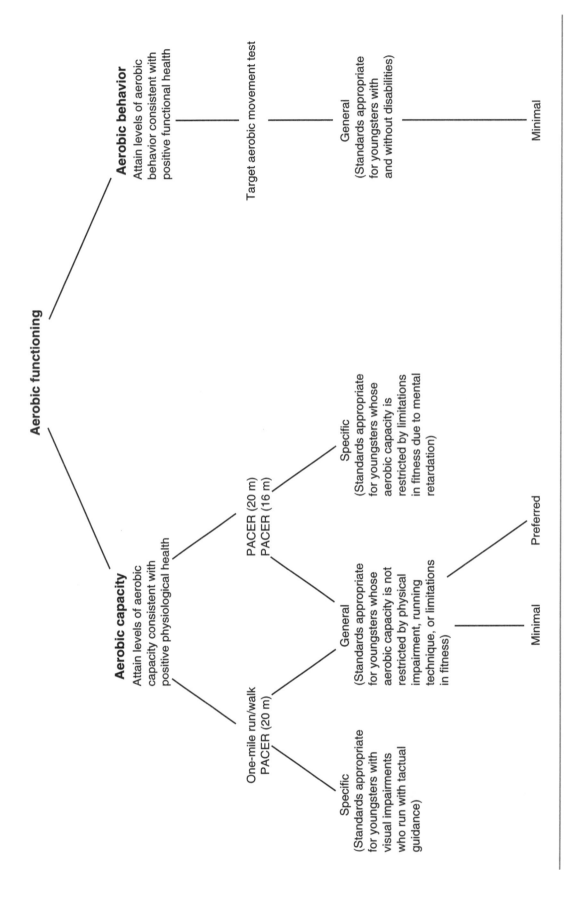

Figure 2.2 Relationships and standards related to aerobic functioning.

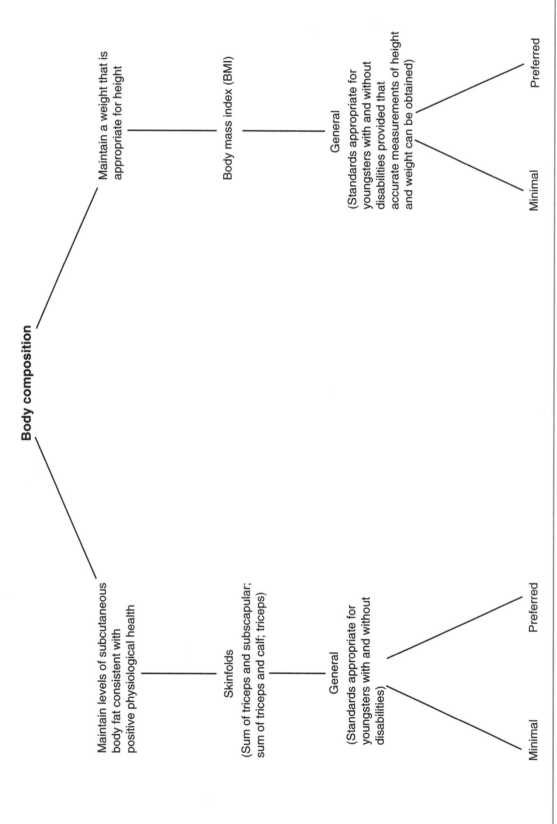

Figure 2.3 Relationships and standards related to body composition.

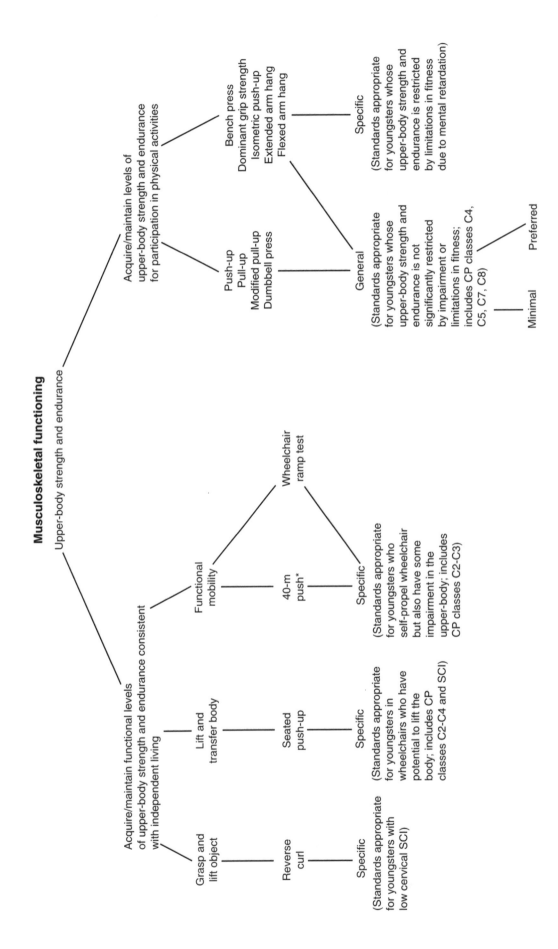

Figure 2.4 Relationships and standards related to upper-body strength and endurance.

*40-m push is used as a general strength and endurance item.

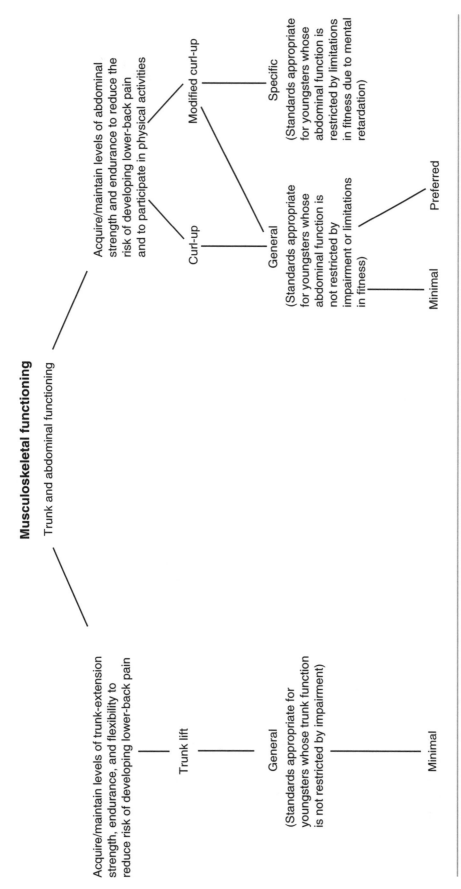

Figure 2.5 Relationships and standards related to trunk and abdominal functioning.

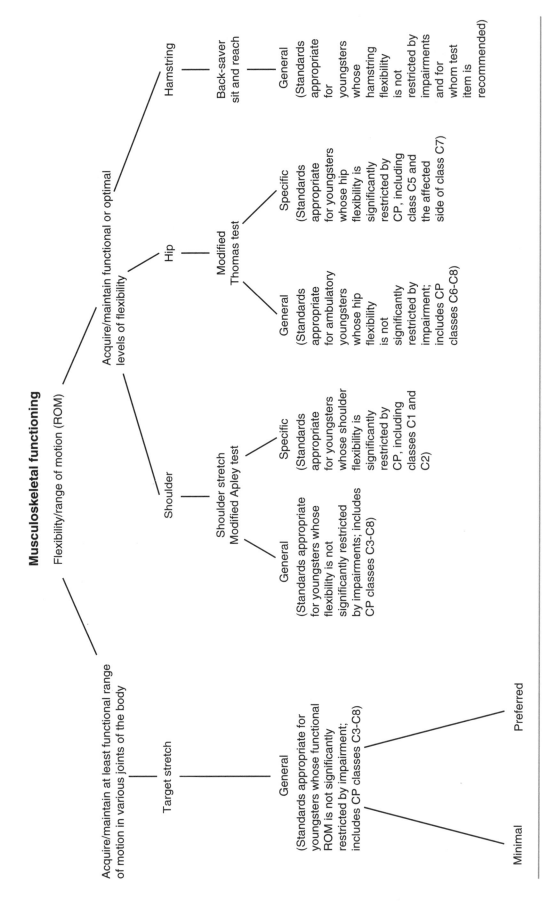

Figure 2.6 Relationships and standards related to flexibility or range of motion.

3

USING THE BROCKPORT PHYSICAL FITNESS TEST

This test manual provides the Brockport Physical Fitness Test and a process for modifying the test for youngsters with unique needs. Components of fitness, profile statements, test items, and standards are suggested for youngsters in targeted populations. For each group covered in this manual, parameters of fitness (components, profiles, tests, and standards) are recommended based on information found in the professional literature or expressed by experts in the field. However, the health-related needs of a particular individual may vary from those of others in a particular group and may require adjustments in the parameters. This chapter provides general information on how to test and evaluate using the BPFT and distinguishes three alternative uses of the BPFT: (1) general procedures, (2) adjustments to general procedures for youngsters with disabilities, and (3) using the BPFT with other tests. The final section of this chapter deals briefly with the development of an individualized education program.

GENERAL PROCEDURES FOR TESTING AND EVALUATING PHYSICAL FITNESS

It is expected that the most common way of using the BPFT will be for testers to adopt the parameters that have been recommended for use with youngsters who have specific disabilities. While such an approach may not reflect the notion of personalization in the strictest sense, there are a number of advantages to this strategy. First, because parameters were developed with specific target populations in mind, they likely are relevant for a youngster in a particular group. Second, each test item included in the battery is considered a valid and reliable health-related measure for members of the target population. Third, standards are recommended based in part on field testing of subjects from the various target populations. Finally, adopting recommended parameters saves the tester time when personalizing the test.

Testers who choose to use the BPFT in this fashion follow a four-step process when administering the test:

1. Accurately classify or subclassify each youngster.
2. Select appropriate test items.
3. Measure physical fitness status by administering test items.
4. Evaluate health-related physical fitness.

The tester's first responsibility is to accurately classify the youngster to be tested according to the disability (e.g., spinal cord injury, blindness). For youngsters with physical disabilities, it also will be necessary to subclassify them according to the nature and extent of their disability. Testers probably will need to consult the "Target Populations" section of chapter 1 to complete this task.

Once the youngster is classified (and subclassified, as necessary), the tester uses the test-item selection guides (tables 4.1 through 4.6 in chapter 4) to choose test items to be administered. When selecting test items in this manner, the tester is implicitly adopting the desired profile written for a specific disability group because the items were derived from the profile statements.

Some test items are recommended and others are optional. A recommended test item is one that relates to a particular component of physical fitness and a specific profile statement and generally is believed to be the "best" test of those parameters for a particular class of youngsters. A recommended item is considered the first choice, but not necessarily the only choice, in test selection. Optional items also address specific components and profile statements and provide additional choices for testers. Testers may select an optional item over a recommended item for any number of reasons, including equipment availability, facility requirements, the youngster's personal characteristics, specific purpose for testing, and so forth. Whether testers choose recommended or optional items, ordinarily the test battery consists of four to six test items: one for aerobic functioning, one for body composition, and two to four for musculoskeletal functioning. Recommended and optional test items and available standards are summarized in table 3.1 for each of the target populations.

The third responsibility of the tester is to measure physical fitness status by administering test items appropriately. Information for this purpose is presented in chapter 5. Chapter 5 provides recommendations for test administration, including necessary equipment, scoring, trials, test modifications, and suggestions for test administration and offers a section on safety guidelines and precautions. After test items are administered, the results are recorded. *The Fitness Challenge: Software for the Brockport Physical Fitness Test* (Short & Winnick, 1999) developed for this test is recommended for this purpose. Also, experienced testers may develop recording systems that work best for them. A sample is provided in form 3.1.

The tester's final responsibility is to evaluate the health-related physical fitness level of each youngster. Youngsters are evaluated by comparing their results on recommended or optional test items with criterion-referenced standards appropriate for them. The derivation of the standards is summarized in chapter 2. The standards themselves appear in tables 4.7 through 4.18 in chapter 4. Again, it is recommended that *The Fitness Challenge: Software for the Brockport Physical Fitness Test* (Short & Winnick, 1999) developed for the BPFT be used to enhance the evaluation of physical fitness.

Both general and specific standards may be available to the tester when evaluating the physical fitness of youngsters with specific disabilities. General stan-

Table 3.1 Summary of Recommended and Optional Test Items With Available Standards

	General population		Mental retardation		Blind with assistance		Cerebral palsy		Spinal cord injury		Congenital anomalies/ amputation	
	Test item	Available standard	Test item	Available standard	Test item	Available standard	Test item	Available standard	Test item	Available standard	Test item	Available standard
Aerobic functioning												
PACER (20 m)	O	G	R†	S	R	S					O†	G
PACER (16 m)			R†	S								
One-mile run/walk	R	G			O†	S					R†	G
TAMT	R	G*	R	G*			R	G*	R	G*	R†	G*
Body composition												
Skinfolds	R	G	R	G	R	G	R	G	R	G	R	G
BMI	O	G	O	G	O	G	O	G				
Musculoskeletal functioning												
Reverse curl									R†	S*		
Seated push-up							R†	S	R†	S	R†	S
40-m push/walk							R†	S*				
Wheelchair ramp test							R†/O†	S*	O†	G		
Bench press		G	O†	S						G	R†	G

(continued)

Table 3.1 *(continued)*

	General population		Mental retardation		Blind with assistance		Cerebral palsy		Spinal cord injury		Congenital anomalies/ amputation	
	Test item	Available standard	Test item	Available standard	Test item	Available standard	Test item	Available standard	Test item	Available standard	Test item	Available standard
Musculoskeletal functioning												
Dumbbell press		G					R†/O†	G	O†	G	R†/O†	G
Extended arm hang		G	R†	S								
Flexed arm hang	O	G	R†	S	O	G	O†	G	R†	G	O†	G
Dominant grip strength		G	O	S								
Isometric push-up		G	O†	S								
Push-up	R	G			R	G						
Pull-up	O	G			O	G						
Modified pull-up	O	G			O	G						
Curl-up	R	G			R	G					R†	G
Modified curl-up			R									
Trunk lift	R	G*	R	G*	R	G*	R†	G*/S*			R†	G*
Modified Apley test		G*							R†	G*	R†	G*
Shoulder stretch	O	G*	O	G*	O	G*	R†	G*/S*				
Modified Thomas test		G*							R†	G*	R†	G*
Back-saver sit and reach	R	G*	R	G*	R	G*					R†	G*
TST		G					R†/O†	G	R†	G	R†	G

R = recommended test item; O = optional test item; G = general standard; S = specific standard

---

* Only single standard is available.

† Item is recommended or optional for some, but not all, members of the category. (Consult test-item selection guides in chapter 4.)

Note: "Blind with assistance" refers to youngsters who are blind and are being assisted in running activities.

dards are available for almost all test items and are recommended when expectations for performance are typical of the general population (i.e., it is believed that a disability does not result in a unique physical fitness need and does not significantly alter performance expectations for the youngster). Specific standards are available only for selected items when it is believed a particular disability dictates an adjustment to general standards for a particular test (or when the test item is unique to a particular disability). Testers should not assume that general standards are not attainable by a youngster within a specific disability category. In fact, testers are encouraged to select general standards, even when specific standards are available, when the general standards are believed to be attainable by a particular youngster.

The evaluation of health-related fitness includes interpretation of results and identification of unique needs, if any. Identified needs may be incorporated into an individualized education program (IEP) for a youngster. Form 3.2 presents a sample test form which reflects this process.

ADJUSTING THE BPFT

Although recommended fitness parameters are likely to pertain to most youngsters from a specific target population, they may not be appropriate for all. In the BPFT, testers always have latitude to adjust the parameters to meet the unique needs of a youngster. Testers may choose to delete, alter, or substitute profile statements related to components of fitness, test items, or standards.

Testers, for instance, may wish to use form 3.3 as a way of personalizing desired profiles for individual youngsters. As an example, a teacher is working with a boy who has a mild form of cerebral palsy. The teacher reviews the fitness parameters recommended for youngsters with cerebral palsy (see chapter 4) and decides to adopt the recommended profile, items, and standards. However, the teacher also would like to include a measure of abdominal strength and endurance for this youngster, even though such a statement is not included in the recommended profile. The teacher could design a new profile by checking all the relevant profile statements in form 3.3, including "Acquire/maintain minimally acceptable levels of abdominal strength and endurance to reduce the risk of developing lower-back pain and to participate in physical activities." The teacher then consults figure 2.5 (p. 29) on trunk and abdominal functioning, finds the appropriate profile statement, selects the relevant test (either curl-ups or modified curl-ups in this case), and either adopts the recommended general standards available for the test or creates individualized standards for the youngster.

In some cases the recommended profile might be appropriate for a youngster, but the recommended or optional test items might not be the best option. Consider a girl who is blind and who also has an additional impairment that results in a significant loss of function in her right arm. The push-up test of upper-body strength and endurance is recommended for youngsters who are blind, but the teacher believes it is inappropriate for this student. Instead, the teacher consults figure 2.4 (p. 28) and selects an alternative measure of upper-body strength and endurance that can be performed using just one side of the body (i.e., dumbbell press or dominant grip strength). The teacher properly decides to use the general standards to assess the strength and endurance of this youngster's left hand or arm.

Whenever testers make adjustments to the general procedures, they are encouraged to use the schematics in figures 2.2 through 2.6 in chapter 2 as a basis for changing either profiles, items, or standards. Of course, testers also are free to develop their own fitness parameters as they deem necessary, but when they do so, they should carefully document the parameters, including the bases for the standards.

Form 3.1 Sample Brockport Physical Fitness Test Form

Student's name: _____ Sex: ☐ M ☐ F Age (yr):_____

Height: _____ Weight: _____ Date: _____

Classification: _____ Subclassification: _____

Test item	Units of measure	Test score	Specific standards	General standards	
				Min.	Pref.
Aerobic functioning					
Aerobic capacity					
Aerobic behavior					
TAMT					
Body Composition					
Skinfold(s):					
Body mass index					
Musculoskeletal functioning					
Strength and endurance					
Flexibility/range of motion					

Interpretation: _____

Needs: _____

Form 3.2 Sample Completed Brockport Physical Fitness Test Form

Student's name: _Leroy Slimmer_ Sex: ☒ M ☐ F Age (yr): _14_

Height: _68 in._ Weight: _150 lb_ Date: _2-17-97_

Classification: _MR—mild limitations_ Subclassification: _NA_

Test item	Units of measure	Test score	Specific standards	General standards	
				Min.	Pref.
Aerobic functioning					
Aerobic capacity					
Aerobic behavior					
TAMT	min	P			P
Body Composition					
Skinfold(s):sum of triceps and subscapular	mm	27		14-31	14-25
Body mass index					
Musculoskeletal functioning					
Strength and endurance					
Dominant grip	kg	25	22	33	42
Flexed arm hang	s	06	08	15	20
Modified curl-up	#	16	14	24	45
Flexibility/range of motion					
Back-saver sit and reach	in.	8			8
Trunk lift	in.	9			9-12

Interpretation: _Meets general standards on TAMT, back saver and trunk lift; meets minimal general standards for body composition; meets specific standards for dominant grip and modified curl-up; fails specific standard for flexed arm hang._

Needs: _Priority 1 - upper body strength/endurance_
Priority 2 - abdominal strength/endurance

Form 3.3 Physical Fitness Profile Sheet

Name: _____ Date: _____

Sex: ☐ M ☐ F Age: _____ Disability: _____

Disability classification: _____

Physical fitness profile: Considering the health-related needs of this student, construct a profile by placing check marks next to those statements that are most relevant to the fitness needs of this youngster. Then select specific test items and standards for measurement and assessment.

AEROBIC FUNCTIONING

Aerobic capacity

☐ Attain levels of aerobic capacity consistent with positive physiological health.

Aerobic behavior

☐ Attain levels of aerobic behavior consistent with positive functional health.

BODY COMPOSITION

Subcutaneous fat

☐ Maintain levels of subcutaneous body fat consistent with positive physiological health.

Weight for height

☐ Maintain a weight that is appropriate for height.

MUSCULOSKELETAL FUNCTIONING

Strength and endurance

☐ Acquire/maintain functional levels of upper-body strength and endurance consistent with independent living: (a) ability to grasp and lift a light weight, (b) ability to lift and transfer the body from a wheelchair, and/or (c) ability to attain functional mobility.

☐ Acquire/maintain levels of upper-body strength and endurance for participation in physical activities.

☐ Acquire/maintain levels of trunk-extension strength, endurance, and flexibility to reduce the risk of developing lower-back pain.

☐ Acquire/maintain levels of abdominal strength and endurance to reduce the risk of developing lower-back pain and to participate in physical activities.

Flexibility or range of motion

☐ Acquire/maintain at least functional range of motion in various joints of the body.

☐ Acquire/maintain functional or optimal levels of flexibility in one or more of the following regions of the body: (a) shoulders, (b) hips, or (c) hamstrings.

USING THE BPFT WITH OTHER TESTS

Youngsters with disabilities are often able to perform one or more of the same test items and achieve the same performance standards as youngsters in the general population. Teachers in inclusive settings, for example, are encouraged to administer the same test items from their regular test battery to youngsters both with and without disabilities when appropriate. There may be times, however, when either the test or standards need to be different for a youngster with a disability. In these circumstances, the BPFT can serve as a reference to fill in gaps that exist in a testing program for a particular youngster. Teachers who use the *FITNESSGRAM* as their regular test battery will find it relatively easy to substitute items, standards, or both from the BPFT because of similarities between these two tests. Regardless of the test a teacher may use, however, the BPFT can be used as a resource for personalization. As another option, those who teach students both with and without disabilities may wish to adopt the BPFT as a single test that can be used for youngsters of the general population as well as those with disabilities.

DEVELOPING AN INDIVIDUALIZED EDUCATION PROGRAM

As a closing thought, teachers should recognize that the personalized approach of the BPFT is consistent with requirements for developing an individualized education program (IEP). Profile statements, with modifications as necessary, can be viewed as annual goals for students' physical fitness. Recent test scores obtained by a youngster can serve as entries under the section on present level of performance of the IEP. General or specific standards can be consulted by the teacher and adopted or modified as performance criteria associated with short-term instructional objectives.

4

PROFILES, TEST SELECTION GUIDES, AND STANDARDS

This chapter presents health-related criterion-referenced parameters, test selection guides, and standards for assessing physical fitness for youngsters in each of the populations targeted by the Brockport Physical Fitness Test. At the end of this chapter are a series of tables presenting standards for assessing health-related, criterion-referenced physical fitness.

Health-Related, Criterion-Referenced Physical Fitness Parameters for Youngsters in the General Population

HEALTH-RELATED CONCERNS

Health-related needs and concerns of youngsters in the general population include avoiding high blood pressure, coronary heart disease, obesity, diabetes, some forms of cancer, and other health problems; lower-back health; and functional health.

DESIRED PROFILE

Boys and girls ages 10 to 17 should possess, at minimum, levels of maximal oxygen uptake and body composition consistent with positive health, flexibility for functional health (especially good functioning of the lower back), and levels of abdominal and upper-body strength and endurance adequate for independent living and participation in physical activities.

COMPONENTS OF PHYSICAL FITNESS

The components of physical fitness are categorized as aerobic functioning, body composition, and musculoskeletal functioning. Test items to assess these components appear in table 4.1.

STANDARDS

Aerobic Functioning

For the general population, aerobic functioning is evaluated using the minimal and preferred general standards presented in table 4.7. The minimal general standard represents the lowest level of $\dot{V}O_2$max consistent with minimizing disease risk and with adequate functioning capacity for daily living. Preferred general standards represent a good level of aerobic capacity associated with a lower disease risk in adults and a higher functional capacity (Cureton, 1994a). The one-mile run/walk and PACER standards presented in table 4.7 correspond to minimal and preferred general $\dot{V}O_2$max standards.

Body Composition

For the general population percentage body fat is evaluated using general standards appearing in tables 4.10 and 4.11. Minimal general standards (table 4.10) for body composition represent minimally acceptable ranges of percentage body fat. The preferred general standards (table 4.11) reflect optimal levels of percentage body fat. Body mass index (BMI) data corresponding to minimal and preferred percentage fat for boys and girls in each targeted age group are also presented in tables 4.10 and 4.11.

Musculoskeletal Functioning

General standards are used to evaluate youngsters in the general population. Minimal muscular strength and endurance standards correspond closely to fitness levels equal to the 20th percentile of the general population, and preferred standards to a fitness level equal to approximately the 60th percentile. Standards are presented in table 4.12 for push-up, pull-up, and modified pull-up. Standards for flexed arm hang are presented in table 4.13 and for curl-up and trunk lift in table 4.16. General standards associated with test items designed to assess flexibility (back saver sit and reach and shoulder stretch) or trunk extension strength and flexibility (trunk lift) are based on normative data and expert judgment as to what represents an acceptable level of function. For the trunk lift, scores beyond 12 in. (30 cm) are discouraged. Standards for test items designed to assess flexibility (back-saver sit and reach and shoulder stretch) are presented in table 4.17.

Table 4.1 Test-Item Selection Guide for Youngsters in the General Population[a]

Fitness component and test item	Selection guide
Aerobic functioning	
Select one:	
One-mile run/walk	R
20-m PACER (recommended for grades K-3)	O
Body composition	
Select one:	
Skinfolds	
Sum of triceps and calf	R
Body mass index (BMI)	O
Musculoskeletal function	
Required:	
Curl-up	R
Trunk lift	R
Select one:	
Push-up	R
Modified pull-up	O
Pull-up	O
Flexed arm hang	O
Select one:	
Back-saver sit and reach	R
Shoulder stretch	O

R = recommended; O = optional

[a]The test items and selection guide for youngsters in the general population presented in this table are adapted with permission from The Cooper Institute for Aerobics Research (CIAR), Dallas, Texas and are based upon the 1992 Prudential *FITNESSGRAM* assessment (CIAR, 1992). In 1999, the *FITNESSGRAM* assessment was revised (CIAR, 1999) to replace the 1992 version. Although not exactly the same, this guide is very consistent with the 1992 edition.

Health-Related, Criterion-Referenced Physical Fitness Parameters for Youngsters With Mental Retardation and Mild Limitations in Physical Fitness

HEALTH-RELATED CONCERNS

Health-related needs and concerns of youngsters with mental retardation and mild limitations in physical fitness include those of youngsters in the general population. Additional concerns relate to inability to sustain aerobic activity, musculoskeletal functioning within acceptable levels, and independent living and participation in daily living activities (including sport and movement activities).

DESIRED PROFILE

Boys and girls ages 10 to 17 with mental retardation and mild limitations in physical fitness should possess, at minimum, levels of aerobic behavior consistent with ability to sustain moderate physical activity or possess a level of aerobic capacity consistent with positive health; body composition consistent with positive health; healthful levels of flexibility or range of motion (especially of the lower back); and levels of abdominal and upper-body strength and endurance appropriate for independent living, participation in physical activities, and progress toward performance levels of peers in the general population.

COMPONENTS OF PHYSICAL FITNESS

Test items to assess aerobic functioning, body composition, and musculoskeletal functioning appear in table 4.2.

STANDARDS

The physical fitness of youngsters with mental retardation is evaluated using specific and general standards. Youngsters attaining general standards related to body composition, aerobic behavior, and flexibility meet minimally acceptable to good health-related levels of physical fitness for the general population. Youngsters meeting specific standards for test items measuring strength or endurance and aerobic capacity attain minimally acceptable levels of physical fitness adjusted for the effects of impairment. These specific standards are initial steps in progressing toward acceptable or good levels of health-related physical fitness for the general population.

Aerobic Functioning

Aerobic capacity for youngsters with mental retardation is evaluated using specific and general standards. Specific standards for $\dot{V}O_2$max and the 16-m and 20-m PACER are presented in table 4.9. Specific standards represent minimally acceptable levels of aerobic capacity adjusted for youngsters with mental retardation. These are based on a 10% adjustment from minimal general standards recommended for youngsters in the general population. Minimal general standards for $\dot{V}O_2$max, the one mile run/walk, and the 16-m and 20-m PACER are presented in table 4.7. These minimal general standards represent the lowest level of $\dot{V}O_2$max consistent with minimizing disease and with adequate functioning for daily living. Aerobic behavior is measured by the TAMT. For the TAMT, performance for 15 min at level 1 is the standard representing ability to sustain moderate physical activity. The same standard exists for all levels of the test. Level 1 is the minimal test level recommended for youngsters with mental retardation and mild limitations in physical fitness.

Table 4.2 Test-Item Selection Guide for Youngsters With Mental Retardation and Mild Limitations in Physical Fitness

Fitness component and test item	Selection guide
Aerobic Functioning	
Select one:	
TAMT (aerobic behavior–level 1)	R
16-m PACER (ages 10-12) *or* 20-m PACER (ages 13-17) (aerobic capacity)	R
Body Composition	
Select one:	
Skinfolds	
Sum of triceps and calf or	R
sum of triceps and subscapular	O
Body mass index	O
Musculoskeletal Function	
Select one:	
Dominant grip strength (ages 10-17)	O
Isometric push-up (10-12), *or* bench press (ages 13-17)	O
Select one:	
Extended arm hang (ages 10-12) *or* flexed arm hang (ages 13-17)	R
Select one:	
Back-saver sit and reach	R
Shoulder stretch	O
Required:	
Modified curl-up	R
Trunk lift	R

R = recommended; O = optional

Body Composition

General standards appearing in tables 4.10 and 4.11 are recommended for evaluation of body composition of youngsters with mental retardation and mild limitations in physical fitness.

Musculoskeletal Functioning

Specific and general standards are used for evaluating dominant grip strength, extended arm hang, isometric push-up, bench press, and flexed arm hang for youngsters with mental retardation and mild limitations in physical fitness. Specific standards reflect minimally acceptable levels of strength or endurance adjusted for mental retardation and are presented in table 4.14. Specific standards for youngsters with mental retardation represent the following percentages of the performances of youngsters in the general population: dominant grip strength, 65%; extended arm hang, 75%; isometric push-up, bench press, flexed arm hang, and modified curl-up, 60%. Youngsters with mental retardation can also be evaluated using minimal and preferred general standards (tables 4.12 and 4.13). Minimal and preferred general standards for the general population for dominant grip, extended arm hang, isometric push-up, and bench press represent the 20th and 60th percentile, respectively, of performance by a Brockport sample of youngsters from the general population. Minimal and preferred general standards for flexed arm hang and modified curl-ups duplicate minimal standards for youngsters from the general population (Cooper Institute for Aerobics Research, 1992 and 1999). It is recommended that general standards reflecting positive levels of physical fitness be used for evaluation of the back-saver sit and reach, trunk lift, and shoulder stretch. These appear in tables 4.16 and 4.17.

Health-Related, Criterion-Referenced Physical Fitness Parameters for Youngsters With Visual Impairments

HEALTH-RELATED CONCERNS

Health-related needs and concerns of youngsters with visual impairments include those of youngsters in the general population and musculoskeletal function necessary for appropriate pelvic alignment and posture.

DESIRED PROFILE

Boys and girls ages 10 to 17 should possess, at minimum, levels of maximal oxygen uptake and body composition consistent with positive health, flexibility for functional health (especially appropriate pelvic alignment and posture and functioning of the lower back), and levels of abdominal and upper-body strength and endurance adequate for independent living and participation in physical activities.

COMPONENTS OF PHYSICAL FITNESS

Test items to assess aerobic functioning, body composition, and musculoskeletal functioning appear in table 4.3.

STANDARDS

Aerobic Functioning

The same standards used for evaluating aerobic functioning of the general population presented in table 4.1 can be used for youngsters with visual impairments with one exception. These specific standards are presented in table 4.8. Specific standards are recommended for youngsters who are blind and require assistance in performing the one-mile run/walk and the 20-m PACER. These specific standards are adjusted 10 percentile points from minimal general standards. General standards may also be used regarding youngsters who are blind and need assistance with running in the one-mile run/walk and the 20-m PACER. Youngsters reaching these standards meet unadjusted general standards for aerobic capacity. Remember that most youngsters with visual impairments can be evaluated using the same general standards used for their sighted peers.

Body Composition

Minimal and preferred general standards for percentage body fat and BMI (tables 4.10 and 4.11) are recommended for youngsters with visual impairments.

Musculoskeletal Functioning

It is recommended that youngsters with visual impairments be evaluated using minimal and preferred general standards. Standards for the curl-up (table 4.16), trunk lift (table 4.16), push-up (table 4.12), pull-up (table 4.12), modified pull-up (table 4.12), and flexed arm hang (table 4.13) reflect the upper and lower values associated with youngsters in the general population. Standards for the back-saver sit and reach and the shoulder stretch (table 4.17) represent levels of musculoskeletal functioning consistent with the general population.

Table 4.3   Test-Item Selection Guide for Youngsters With Visual Impairments

Fitness component and test item	Selection guide
Aerobic functioning	
Aerobic capacity	
Select one:	
20-m PACER (ages 10-17)	R
One mile run/walk (ages 15-17)	O
Body composition	
Select one:	
Skinfolds	
Sum of triceps and calf	R
Body mass index	O
Musculoskeletal function	
Required:	
Curl-up	R
Trunk lift	R
Select one:	
Push-up	R
Pull-up	O
Modified pull-up	O
Flexed arm hang	O
Select one:	
Back-saver sit and reach	R
Shoulder stretch	O

R = recommended; O = optional

Health-Related, Criterion-Referenced Physical Fitness Parameters for Youngsters With Spinal Cord Injuries

HEALTH-RELATED CONCERNS

Health-related needs and concerns typical of youngsters with spinal cord injuries include those of youngsters in the general population; inability to sustain aerobic activity; lack of flexibility or range of motion of the hips and upper body, particularly the shoulder; lack of strength and endurance to lift and transfer the body independently, lift the body to prevent decubitus ulcers, and propel a wheelchair; and excessive body fat, which inhibits health.

DESIRED PROFILE

Individuals with spinal cord injuries should possess, at minimum, the ability to sustain moderate physical activity, body composition consistent with positive health, levels of flexibility and range of motion to perform activities of daily living and to inhibit contractures, levels of muscular strength and endurance for wheelchair users to lift and transfer the body and push a wheelchair, muscular strength and endurance to counteract muscular weaknesses, and fitness levels needed to enhance the performance of daily living activities (including sport activities).

COMPONENTS OF PHYSICAL FITNESS

Test items to assess aerobic functioning, body composition, and musculoskeletal functioning appear in table 4.4.

STANDARDS

Standards recommended for evaluation pertain only to the test items in table 4.4 designated as recommended or optional for a specific class of youngsters.

Aerobic Functioning

For youngsters with spinal cord injuries aerobic behavior is measured using the TAMT. Completion of level 1 of the test for 15 min represents ability to sustain moderate physical ability and is the recommended general standard for the test.

Body Composition

Minimal and preferred general standards associated with percentage body fat are recommended for evaluating body composition. The specific tables to use depend on the skinfold sites used for testing. Minimal general standards represent minimally acceptable levels of body fat (table 4.10). Preferred general standards represent optimal levels of body fat (table 4.11). The BMI test item is not recommended for youngsters with spinal cord injuries.

Table 4.4 Test-Item Selection Guide for Youngsters With Spinal Cord Injuries

Fitness component and test item	Selection guide		
	LLQ Low-level (C6-C8) quadriplegic	**SCI-PW Paraplegic– wheelchair**	**SCI-PA Paraplegic– ambulatory**
Aerobic functioning			
TAMT (level 1)	R	R	R
Body composition			
Select one:			
Skinfolds			
Sum of triceps and subscapular or	R	R	R
triceps only	O	O	O
Musculoskeletal function			
Required (if appropriate):			
Seated push-up	O/TA[a]	R	
Select one:			
Reverse curl	R		
Dominant grip strength		R	R
Bench press (ages 13-17) or			
dumbbell press (dominant)			
(ages 13-17)		O	O
Select recommended tests:			
Modified Apley test		R	R
Modified Thomas test			R
TST[b]	R	R[c]	

R = recommended; O = optional; TA = task analysis

[a] Task analysis of test items of muscular strength and endurance or variations of test items that reflect the needs and abilities of individual.

[b] Select at least two items from the TST on the basis of possible participant needs. For LLQ shoulder abduction, shoulder external rotation, and forearm pronation are recommended. For SCI-PW and SCI-PA, shoulder abduction and shoulder external rotation are recommended if the modified Apley test is not passed. Measure both extremities on the modified Apley, modified Thomas, and TST, and apply health-related standards as appropriate.

[c] Recommended if the modified Apley test is not passed with a score of 3.

Musculoskeletal Functioning

Musculoskeletal functioning is evaluated using a variety of standards. Minimal and preferred general standards for dominant grip strength, bench press, and dumbbell press are based on 20th and 60th percentile values, respectively, of a sample of youngsters from the general population (tables 4.12 and 4.13). The 5-s specific standard for the seated push-up (table 4.15) is related to the recommendation that wheelchair users should relieve skin pressure in their buttocks and legs for at least 5 s every 15 min. The 20-s standard (table 4.15) is a higher level of strength and endurance that enhances lifting and transferring the body and wheelchair propulsion. The specific standard for the reverse curl is tied directly to the functional ability of lifting a 1-lb (0.5-kg) weight one time (table 4.15). General standards for the modified Apley and Thomas tests (a score of 3) indicate that youngsters have optimal flexibility of the shoulder joint and optimal hip extension, respectively (table 4.17). A score of 1 on TST items is a functional range of motion in a joint (table 4.17). A score of 2 is preferred, reflecting optimal flexibility in a joint. TST standards are general standards.

Health-Related, Criterion-Referenced Physical Fitness Parameters for Youngsters With Cerebral Palsy

HEALTH-RELATED CONCERNS

Health-related needs and concerns of youngsters with cerebral palsy include those typical for youngsters in the general population; the inability to sustain aerobic activity; lack of flexibility or range of motion in various joints of the body; insufficient muscular strength and endurance to maintain muscular balance and body symmetry; inability to engage in independent mobility, lift and transfer the body, perform activities of daily living, and participate in leisure activities; and avoiding either excessive or insufficient body fat, which inhibits health.

DESIRED PROFILE

Individuals with cerebral palsy should possess, at minimum, the ability to sustain moderate physical activity; body composition consistent with positive health; and levels of flexibility and muscular strength and endurance to foster independent living (including mobility), muscle balance and body symmetry, and participation in a variety of physical activities (including sport or leisure activities).

COMPONENTS OF PHYSICAL FITNESS

Test items to assess aerobic functioning, body composition, and musculoskeletal functioning appear in table 4.5.

STANDARDS

Standards recommended for evaluation pertain only to test items designated as recommended or optional. Musculoskeletal functioning standards may be associated with specific classifications. Youngsters with cerebral palsy are required to attain standards on only one side of the body (i.e., dominant or preferred side) for the following items: modified Apley test, TST, dumbbell press, and dominant grip strength.

Aerobic Functioning

For youngsters with cerebral palsy, aerobic behavior is measured using the TAMT. Completion of level 1 of the test for 15 min represents ability to sustain moderate physical activity and is the recommended general standard.

Body Composition

Minimal and preferred general standards for percentage body fat are recommended for youngsters who have cerebral palsy. Minimal general standards represent minimally acceptable levels of body fat (table 4.10). Preferred general standards represent optimal levels of body fat (table 4.11). Values for both sum of triceps and

Table 4.5 Test-Item Selection Guide for Youngsters With Cerebral Palsy

Fitness component and test item	Motorized wheelchair C1[a]	Wheelchair C2U[b]	Wheelchair C2L[b]	Wheelchair C3	Wheelchair C4	Wheelchair C5	Ambulatory C6	Ambulatory C7	Ambulatory C8
Aerobic functioning									
TAMT (level 1)	R	R	R	R	R	R	R	R	R
Body composition									
Select one:									
Skinfolds									
Sum of triceps and subscapular	R	R	R	R	R	R	R	R	R
Triceps only	O	O	O	O	O	O	O	O	O
Body mass index	O	O	O	O	O	O	O	O	O
Musculoskeletal function									
Select one or more:									
Modified Apley test[c,d]	R	R		R	R	R	R	R	R
Modified Thomas test[c]						R	R	R	R
TST[e]	R	R	R	R	R	O	O	O	O
Select one or more (except for C1)[a]:									
Seated push-up[f]		R		R	R		R		
40-m wheelchair push		R	R	O					
Dominant grip strength					O	O		O	O
Dumbbell press (dominant) (ages 13-17)				O	O	O		R	R
40-m walk							R		
Wheelchair ramp test				R					

R = recommended; O = optional

[a] If recommended test items are inappropriate for individuals classified as C1, it is recommended that these test items or alternatives important to the individual be task analyzed and used in connection with individual developmental progress.

[b] C2 participants with a higher degree of functioning in the upper extremities are classified 2U, and those with a higher degree of functioning in the lower extremities are classified 2L.

[c] Test one or both extremities, as appropriate.

[d] Omit this item for C1 subjects using assistive devices.

[e] Test items should be administered on right and left extremities, as appropriate. TST items particularly important for people with cerebral palsy include elbow and shoulder extension, shoulder abduction, shoulder external rotation, and forearm supination. For ambulatory people, knee extension measurements may be particularly important.

[f] Test item not recommended for hemiplegic C3 and C4 participants. Hemiplegic participants should be given the dumbbell press.

subscapular skinfolds and body mass index relate to these body fat ranges. The BMI should be used only if height and weight can be measured accurately.

Musculoskeletal Functioning

Musculoskeletal functioning is evaluated using a variety of standards. Minimal and preferred general standards for dominant grip and dumbbell press are based on 20th and 60th percentile values, respectively, of a sample of youngsters from the general population (table 4.12). The standard for the 40-m push/walk (table 4.15) is suggested for functional mobility, which reflects a minimal level of musculoskeletal ability involving strength, endurance, and flexibility. The 5-s specific standard for the seated push-up (table 4.15) is related to the recommendation that wheelchair users should relieve the skin pressure on their buttocks and legs for at least 5 s every 15 min. The 20-s specific standard represents a higher level of strength and endurance, which enhances muscular balance around the elbow, ability to transfer the body, and ability to propel a wheelchair.

The wheelchair ramp test 8-foot specific standards reflect the ability to ascend a ramp with approximately one step of elevation (8 inches) such as would be found at a corner curb-cut. The 15-foot specific standard can vary between 15 and 30 inches of rise in elevation (at the discretion of the tester) as a function of the length of a ramp a youngster might frequently encounter in their environment.

Standards for the modified Apley test, modified Thomas test, and TST vary for each classification. Modified Apley test standards (tables 4.17 and 4.18) are derived on a logical basis (see chapter 2 for description). The general standard for the modified Apley test (a score of 3) is recommended for youngsters in classes C2U to C8. A specific standard of 2 is recommended for classes C1 and C2L. Modified Thomas test standards (tables 4.17 and 4.18) relate to flexibility of the hip flexors. The general standard for the modified Thomas test (a score of 3) is recommended for youngsters in classes C6 and C8. A specific standard of 2 is recommended for class C5. For class C7 (hemiplegia), a score of 3 is recommended for the unaffected side, while a score of 2 is recommended for the affected side of the body. The TST standard for youngsters in most classes (C3-C8) is the minimal general standard (a score of 1; table 4.17), which represents a clinically accepted functional range of motion in a joint. The preferred general standard (a score of 2) represents optimal range of motion for a particular joint. The TST is also recommended for classes C1 and C2; however, individualized rather than health-related general standards are recommended for these classes. It should be noted that standards for the modified Apley test and TST for youngsters with cerebral palsy are applied to the dominant or preferred side of the body.

Health-Related, Criterion-Referenced Physical Fitness Parameters for Youngsters With Congenital Anomalies and Amputations

HEALTH-RELATED CONCERNS

Health-related needs and concerns of youngsters with congenital anomalies and amputations include those typical of youngsters in the general population; inability to sustain aerobic activity; lack of upper- and lower-body flexibility or range of motion; lack of muscular strength and endurance of wheelchair users to lift and transfer the body independently; inability to overcome architectural barriers, lift the body to prevent decubitus ulcers, and propel a wheelchair; and avoiding excessive body fat, which inhibits health.

DESIRED PROFILE

Individuals with congenital anomalies and amputations should possess, at minimum and as appropriate, the ability to sustain moderate physical activity and/or physical activity that promotes levels of functioning consistent with positive health; body composition consistent with positive health; levels of flexibility and range of motion to perform activities of daily living and to inhibit contractures; levels of muscular strength and endurance of wheelchair users to lift and transfer the body, overcome architectural barriers, and propel a wheelchair; abdominal and upper-body muscular strength and endurance to counteract muscular weakness; and fitness levels needed to enhance performance of daily living activities (including sport and movement activities).

COMPONENTS OF PHYSICAL FITNESS

Test items to assess aerobic functioning, body composition, and musculoskeletal functioning appear in table 4.6.

STANDARDS

Standards recommended for evaluation pertain only to test items in table 4.6 designated as recommended or optional.

Aerobic Functioning

Aerobic behavior is measured using the TAMT. Completion of level 1 of the test for 15 min represents ability to sustain moderate physical activity and is the recommended minimal general standard for the test. Minimal and preferred general standards for $\dot{V}O_2$max, one-mile run/walk, and PACER—measures of aerobic capacity—are presented in table 4.7.

Body Composition

Minimal and preferred general standards for percentage body fat are used. Skinfold measurements corresponding to these standards are presented in tables 4.10 and 4.11.

Musculoskeletal Functioning

Musculoskeletal functioning is evaluated using a variety of standards. Minimal and preferred general standards for dominant grip strength, dumbbell press, and bench press are based on 20th and 60th percentile values, respectively, of the Brockport sample of youngsters from the general population (tables 4.12 and 4.13). Minimal and preferred general standards for the curl-up (table 4.16), trunk lift (table 4.16) correspond respectively to upper and lower values associated with standards for youngsters in the general population. These standards are associated with *FITNESSGRAM* standards (Cooper Institute for Aerobics Research, 1992 and 1999). For subclassifications of people for whom the shoulder stretch, back-saver sit and reach, and modified Apley test are recommended for unaffected limbs, the minimal general standards presented in table 4.17 are recommended for evaluation. Standards for these items reflect acceptable levels of flexibility. No distinction between minimal and preferred general standards are given for these items.

As indicated in table 4.6, selected items on the TST are recommended for various subclassifications. If potential is not limited by an impairment, target scores of 1 or above should be attainable. If an impairment affects extent of movement, the TST may be used to obtain scores that can be used to determine present individual status and progress. A score of 1 is the minimal general standard reflecting functional range of motion, and a score of 2 is the preferred general standard reflecting optimal range of motion (table 4.17).

Table 4.6 Test-Item Selection Guide for Youngsters With Congenital Anomalies and Amputations

Fitness component and test item	Selection guide					
	Subclassification					
	One arm only	Two arms only	One leg only	Two legs only	One arm, one leg (same side)	One arm, one leg (opposite side)
Aerobic functioning						
Select one:						
One-mile run/walk (aerobic capacity)	R	R				
20-m PACER (aerobic capacity)	O	O				
TAMT (level 1) (aerobic behavior)			R	R	R	R
Body composition						
Select one:						
Skinfolds						
Triceps only	R	R[a]	R	R	R	R

Table 4.6

Fitness component and test item	One arm only	Two arms only	One leg only	Two legs only	One arm, one leg (same side)	One arm, one leg (opposite side)
Sum of triceps and subscapular	O	O	R	R	R	R
Sum of triceps and calf	R	R	O		O	O
Musculoskeletal function						
Select one:						
Unaffected limb(s): Shoulder stretch or modified Apley test	R		R	R	R	R
Back-saver sit and reach	R		R		R	
Select as needed:						
Affected limb(s): TST[b]						
Knee extension			O[c,d,e]	O[c,d,e]	O[c,d,e]	O[c,d,e]
Shoulder flexion	O[d,e]	O[d,e]			O[d,e]	O[d,e]
External shoulder rotation	O[d,e]	O[d,e]			O[d,e]	O[d,e]
Elbow extension	O[d,e]	O[d,e]			R[d,e]	R[d,e]
Required:						
Trunk lift	R	R				
Curl-up	R	R				
Select one:						
Dumbbell press (dominant) (ages 13-17)	R		O	O	R	R
Bench press (ages 13-17)			R	R		
Seated push-up			R[f]	R[f]		
Dominant grip strength	O		O	O	O	O

[a] Selection depends on site of anomaly or amputation.

[b] If additional unique range-of-motion needs are suspected, relevant joints may be tested using the TST.

[c] Optional for below-knee amputation or anomaly of affected limb(s) only.

[d] Optional in cases where measurement is possible and appropriate.

[e] If potential is not limited by impairment, target scores of 1 or above on the TST are attainable. If impairment affects extent of movement, the TST may be used to obtain scores from which to determine individual status and progress.

[f] Recommended only for wheelchair users.

Table 4.7 $\dot{V}O_2$max, One-Mile Run/Walk, 20-m PACER, 16-m PACER and Target Aerobic Movement Test: General Standards

	$\dot{V}O_2$max[b] (ml/kg^{-1}/ min^{-1})		One-mile run/walk[b] (min:s)		20-m PACER[b] (# laps)		16-m PACER (# laps)	TAMT[a] (min)
Age	M	P	M	P	M	P	M	M
Males								
10	42	52	11:30	9:00	17	55	25	Pass
11	42	52	11:00	8:30	23	61	33	Pass
12	42	52	10:30	8:00	29	68	40	Pass
13	42	52	10:00	7:30	35	74	48	Pass
14	42	52	9:30	7:00	41	80	55	Pass
15	42	52	9:00	7:00	46	85	61	Pass
16	42	52	8:30	7:00	52	90	69	Pass
17	42	52	8:30	7:00	57	94	75	Pass
Females								
10	39	47	12:30	9:30	7	35	13	Pass
11	38	46	12:00	9:00	9	37	15	Pass
12	37	45	12:00	9:00	13	40	20	Pass
13	36	44	11:30	9:00	15	42	23	Pass
14	35	43	11:00	8:30	18	44	26	Pass
15	35	43	10:30	8:00	23	50	33	Pass
16	35	43	10:00	8:00	28	56	39	Pass
17	35	43	10:00	8:00	34	61	46	Pass

M = minimal standard; P = preferred standard

[a] Scored as pass/fail. Youngsters pass when they sustain moderate physical activity for 15 minutes.

[b] Adapted, with permission, from The Cooper Institute for Aerobics Research, 1992 and 1999, *FITNESSGRAM*, (Dallas, Texas: Cooper Institute for Aerobics Research).

Table 4.8 $\dot{V}O_2$max, One-Mile Run/Walk, 20-m PACER: Specific Standards for Youngsters Who Are Blind

Age	Minimal general $\dot{V}O_2$max ($ml \cdot kg^{-1} \cdot min^{-1}$)	Aerobic capacity	
		One-mile run/walk (min:s)[a]	20-m PACER (# laps)[a]
Males			
10	42	12:30	15
11	42	12:00	21
12	42	11:30	26
13	42	11:00	32
14	42	10:30	37
15	42	10:00	41
16	42	9:30	47
17	42	9:30	51
Females			
10	39	13:30	6
11	38	13:00	8
12	37	13:00	12
13	36	12:00	14
14	35	11:30	17
15	35	11:00	22
16	35	10:30	27
17	35	10:30	32

[a] These specific standards include a bonus of 10 percentile points given to youngsters who are blind and require physical assistance in performing runs. The $\dot{V}O_2$max values associated with these specific standards are the same as the minimal general standards.

Table 4.9 $\dot{V}O_2$max and PACER: Specific Standards for Youngsters With Mental Retardation

Age	$\dot{V}O_2$max (ml · kg^{-1} · min^1) [b]	20-m PACER (# laps) [a]	16-m PACER (# laps) [a]
Males			
10	38	4	9
11	38	10	16
12	38	16	24
13	38	21	30
14	38	27	38
15	38	33	45
16	38	38	57
17	38	44	59
Females			
10	35	1	5
11	34	1	5
12	33	1	5
13	32	4	9
14	31	6	11
15	31	12	19
16	31	17	25
17	31	22	31

[a] 16-m PACER lap scores are extrapolated from 20-m PACER lap scores: 16-m laps = 1.25 (20-m laps) + 3.8, SE = 7.4; 20-m laps = 0.71 (16-m laps) − 0.87, SE = 5.5. 20-m lap values are approximately 63% of 16-m lap scores.

[b] Specific standards associated with a 10% downward adjustment of $\dot{V}O_2$max from minimal general standards, however, the lap standards for 10- and 11-year old girls represent a slightly higher $\dot{V}O_2$max value than shown here.

Table 4.10 Percentage Body Fat, Skinfold, and Body Mass Index:
Minimal General Standards

Age	% fat[a]		Triceps plus subscapular skinfold (mm)		Triceps plus calf skinfold (mm)		Triceps skinfold (mm)		Body mass index[a]	
	U	L	U	L	U	L	U	L	U	L
Males										
10	10	25	11	28	12	33	7	19	15.3	21.0
11	10	25	12	29	12	33	7	19	15.8	21.0
12	10	25	13	30	12	33	7	19	16.0	22.0
13	10	25	13	30	12	33	7	18	16.6	23.0
14	10	25	14	31	12	33	7	18	17.5	24.5
15	10	25	14	32	12	33	7	17	18.1	25.0
16	10	25	15	33	12	33	7	17	18.5	26.5
17	10	25	15	33	12	33	7	16	18.8	27.0
Females										
10	17	32	18	41	20	44	10	24	16.6	23.5
11	17	32	18	41	20	44	10	24	16.9	24.0
12	17	32	18	41	20	44	10	24	16.9	24.5
13	17	32	18	41	20	44	10	23	17.5	24.5
14	17	32	18	41	20	44	10	23	17.5	25.0
15	17	32	18	41	20	44	10	23	17.5	25.0
16	17	32	18	41	20	44	10	22	17.5	25.0
17	17	32	18	41	20	44	10	22	17.5	26.0

U = upper boundary; L = lower boundary

[a] Adapted, with permission, from The Cooper Institute for Aerobics Research, 1992 and 1999, *FITNESSGRAM*, (Dallas, Texas: Cooper Institute for Aerobics Research).

Table 4.11   Percentage Body Fat, Skinfold, and Body Mass Index: Preferred General Standards

Age	% fat		Triceps plus subscapular skinfold (mm)		Triceps plus calf skinfold (mm)		Triceps skinfold (mm)		Body mass index	
	U	L	U	L	U	L	U	L	U	L
Males										
10	10	20	11	22	12	26	7	16	15.3	20.0
11	10	20	12	23	12	26	7	16	15.8	20.0
12	10	20	13	24	12	26	7	16	16.0	20.5
13	10	20	13	24	12	26	7	15	16.6	22.0
14	10	20	14	25	12	26	7	15	17.5	23.0
15	10	20	14	25	12	26	7	14	18.1	24.0
16	10	20	15	26	12	26	7	14	18.5	25.0
17	10	20	15	26	12	26	7	14	18.8	25.5
Females										
10	17	25	18	30	20	33	10	19	16.6	21.5
11	17	25	18	30	20	33	10	19	16.9	22.0
12	17	25	18	30	20	33	10	19	16.9	23.0
13	17	25	18	30	20	33	10	19	17.5	23.0
14	17	25	18	30	20	33	10	19	17.5	23.0
15	17	25	18	30	20	33	10	19	17.5	23.0
16	17	25	18	30	20	33	10	18	17.5	23.5
17	17	25	18	30	20	33	10	18	17.5	23.5

U = upper boundary; L = lower boundary

Table 4.12 Dumbbell Press, Push-Up, Pull-Up, and Modified Pull-Up: General Standards

Age	Dumbbell press (# completed)		Push-up[a] (# completed)		Pull-up[a] (# completed)		Modified pull-up[a] (# completed)	
	M	P	M	P	M	P	M	P
Males								
10			7	20	1	2	5	15
11			8	20	1	3	6	17
12			10	20	1	3	7	20
13	14	22	12	25	1	4	8	22
14	19	28	14	30	2	5	9	25
15	21	33	16	35	3	7	10	27
16	24	39	18	35	5	8	12	30
17	27	45	18	35	5	8	14	30
Females								
10			7	15	1	2	4	13
11			7	15	1	2	4	13
12			7	15	1	2	4	13
13	5	12	7	15	1	2	4	13
14	7	14	7	15	1	2	4	13
15	10	16	7	15	1	2	4	13
16	11	16	7	15	1	2	4	13
17	11	16	7	15	1	2	4	13

M = minimal standard; P = preferred standard

[a] Adapted, with permission, from The Cooper Institute for Aerobics Research, 1992 and 1999, *FITNESSGRAM*, (Dallas, Texas: Cooper Institute for Aerobics Research).

Table 4.13   Isometric Push-Up, Bench Press, Extended Arm Hang, Flexed Arm Hang, and Dominant Grip Strength: General Standards

Age	Isometric push-up (s)		Bench press (# completed)		Extended arm hang (s)		Flexed arm hang[a] (s)		Dominant grip strength (kg)	
	M	P	M	P	M	P	M	P	M	P
Males										
10	**40**	40			**30**	40	**4**	10	**18**	22
11	**40**	40			**30**	40	**6**	13	**21**	26
12	**40**	40			**30**	40	**10**	15	**25**	30
13			**20**	34			**12**	17	**29**	35
14			**33**	43			**15**	20	**33**	42
15			**40**	50			**15**	20	**37**	46
16			**47**	50			**15**	20	**43**	51
17			**50**	50			**15**	20	**49**	57
Females										
10	**25**	40			**20**	40	**4**	10	**17**	20
11	**25**	40			**20**	40	**6**	12	**19**	22
12	**25**	40			**20**	40	**7**	12	**22**	24
13			**10**	23			**8**	12	**24**	28
14			**13**	26			**8**	12	**26**	31
15			**14**	27			**8**	12	**29**	33
16			**14**	27			**8**	12	**29**	33
17			**15**	30			**8**	12	**29**	33

M = minimal standard; P = preferred standard

[a] Adapted, with permission, from The Cooper Institute for Aerobics Research, 1992 and 1999, *FITNESSGRAM*, (Dallas, Texas: Cooper Institute for Aerobics Research).

Table 4.14 Isometric Push-Up, Bench Press, Extended Arm Hang, Flexed Arm Hang, and Dominant Grip Strength: Specific Standards for Youngsters With Mental Retardation

Age	Isometric push-up[a] (s)	Bench press[a] (# completed)	Extended arm hang[b] (s)	Flexed arm hang[a] (s)	Dominant grip strength[c] (kg)
Males					
10	20		23		12
11	20		23		14
12	20		23		16
13		10		6	19
14		16		8	22
15		20		8	24
16		23		8	28
17		25		8	32
Females					
10	13		15		11
11	13		15		12
12	13		15		14
13		5		4	16
14		6		4	17
15		7		4	19
16		7		4	19
17		8		4	19

[a] Specific standards reflect a 50% adjustment to minimal general standards.

[b] Specific standards are 75% of minimal general standards.

[c] Specific standards are 65% of minimal general standards.

Table 4.15 **Reverse Curl, Seated Push-Up, 40-m Push/Walk, and Wheelchair Ramp Test: Specific Standards for Youngsters With Orthopedic Disabilities (Cerebral Palsy and Spinal Cord Injury)**

Age	Reverse curl[a] (# completed)	Seated push-up[b] (s)	40-m push/walk[c] (s)	Wheelchair ramp test[e] (ft)/(m)	
Males and females					
10-17	1	5/20	Pass[d]	8 or ≥ 15	2.4 or ≥ 4.5

[a] Specific standard is appropriate for youngsters with low-level cervical spinal cord injuries (LLQ).

[b] Specific standards are appropriate for youngsters in wheelchairs who have the potential to lift the body (C2-C4, SC1-PW). The 5-s standard should be selected if the functional health concern is with pressure sores and short-term transfer needs. The 20-s standard should be selected if the functional health concern is with longer strength and endurance needs.

[c] Specific standard is appropriate for youngsters who self-propel a wheelchair, but who also have some upper body impairment (C2,C3).

[d] Youngsters pass when they cover the distance within 60 seconds at the acceptable heart-rate intensity.

[e] Scores are pass/fail based upon successful negotiation of 8 foot ramps or ≥ 15 ft ramps.

Table 4.16 Trunk Lift, Curl-Up, and Modified Curl-Up: General Standards and Modified Curl-up: Specific Standards for Youngsters With Mental Retardation

Age	General standards						Specific standards
	Trunk lift[a,b]				Curl-ups and modified curl-ups[b] (# completed)		Modified curl-ups[c] (# completed)
	L (in.)	L (cm)	U (in.)	U (cm)	M	P	
Males							
10	9	23	12	30	12	24	7
11	9	23	12	30	15	28	9
12	9	23	12	30	18	36	11
13	9	23	12	30	21	40	13
14	9	23	12	30	24	45	14
15	9	23	12	30	24	47	14
16	9	23	12	30	24	47	14
17	9	23	12	30	24	47	14
Females							
10	9	23	12	30	12	26	7
11	9	23	12	30	15	29	9
12	9	23	12	30	18	32	11
13	9	23	12	30	18	32	11
14	9	23	12	30	18	32	11
15	9	23	12	30	18	35	11
16	9	23	12	30	18	35	11
17	9	23	12	30	18	35	11

M = minimal standard; P = preferred standard
L = lower boundary of accepted range; U = upper boundary of accepted range

[a] Scores higher than 12 in. or 30 cm should not be encouraged.

[b] Based on standards provided by the Cooper Institute for Aerobics Research, 1992 and 1999.

[c] Specific standard is 60% of minimal general standard for curl-ups.

Table 4.17 Shoulder Stretch, Modified Apley Test, Modified Thomas Test, Back-Saver Sit and Reach, and Target Stretch Test: General Standards

Age	Shoulder stretch[a] (Pass/Fail)	Modified Apley test	Modified Thomas test	Back-saver sit and reach[a] (in.)	(cm)	Target stretch test	
Males							
10	Pass	3	3	8	20	1	2
11	Pass	3	3	8	20	1	2
12	Pass	3	3	8	20	1	2
13	Pass	3	3	8	20	1	2
14	Pass	3	3	8	20	1	2
15	Pass	3	3	8	20	1	2
16	Pass	3	3	8	20	1	2
17	Pass	3	3	8	20	1	2
Females							
10	Pass	3	3	9	23	1	2
11	Pass	3	3	10	25	1	2
12	Pass	3	3	10	25	1	2
13	Pass	3	3	10	25	1	2
14	Pass	3	3	10	25	1	2
15	Pass	3	3	12	30	1	2
16	Pass	3	3	12	30	1	2
17	Pass	3	3	12	30	1	2

[a] Adapted, with permission, from The Cooper Institute for Aerobics Research, 1992 and 1999, *FITNESSGRAM*, (Dallas, Texas: Cooper Institute for Aerobics Research).

Table 4.18   Modified Apley and Thomas Tests: Specific Standards for Youngsters With Cerebral Palsy

Age	Modified Apley test C1 and C2L[a]	Modified Thomas test C5 and C7 (affected side)[a]
Males and females		
10	2	2
11	2	2
12	2	2
13	2	2
14	2	2
15	2	2
16	2	2
17	2	2

[a]When these test items are recommended for other classes of cerebral palsy, use general standards.

5

TEST ADMINISTRATION AND TEST ITEMS

This chapter presents test items in the Brockport Physical Fitness Test in detail. Specific recommendations for administering most test items are also presented. Although the BPFT includes 27 test items, generally only 4 to 6 test items are administered to a particular individual. Following are general recommendations for the administration of the BPFT.

- Practice administering test items and be confident of your mastery in administering them before taking formal measurements.
- Develop forms for selecting test items and for recording scores or use materials developed as a part of *The Fitness Challenge: Software for the Brockport Physical Fitness Test Manual* (Short & Winnick, 1999).
- Describe the test to participants and explain what it is intended to assess.
- Have youngsters dress appropriately. Gym suits and sneakers (where appropriate) are recommended.
- Plan and provide general and specific warm-up as appropriate. This is particularly important when flexibility or range of motion and strenuous effort are involved in test items.
- Provide cool-down activities after testing. This is especially important after aerobic-functioning test items.

The BPFT for youngsters with disabilities was designed to correspond as closely as possible to health-related, criterion-referenced tests for nondisabled youngsters. The BPFT corresponds most closely to Prudential *FITNESSGRAM* and *FITNESSGRAM*. To enhance consistency, the procedures for the following test items were adapted from *The Prudential FITNESSGRAM Test Administration Manual* (Cooper Institute for Aerobics Research, 1992) with permission from The Cooper Institute for Aerobics Research, Dallas, Texas: 20-m PACER, one-mile run/walk, skinfolds, body mass index, curl-up, flexed arm hang, pull-up, modified pull-up, push-up, shoulder stretch, trunk lift, and back-saver sit and reach.

- Provide a positive testing atmosphere. Encourage youngsters to try their best and continually provide positive reinforcement for effort.
- Compare the performance of participants with criterion-referenced standards rather than with other youngsters' performances.
- Administer no more than one half of the items in one particular day. If fatigue appears to be influencing performance, provide longer rest intervals between test items.
- Administer aerobic-functioning tests last.
- Administer running items on flat, hard, yet resilient surfaces.
- Provide participants who are blind the opportunity to become clearly oriented to a test station or testing area. This is particularly important for tests involving running.
- Provide careful demonstrations for participants with hearing impairments. Give instructions in writing or manually (e.g., signing, finger spelling). Use hand signals to start and stop activities.
- Administer the following test items individually to one participant at a time: TAMT, skinfolds, extended arm hang, flexed arm hang, modified pull-up, pull-up, dominant grip strength, bench press, curl-up, modified curl-up, 40-m push/walk, reverse curl, seated push-up, trunk lift, wheelchair ramp test, and most flexibility or range-of-motion test items (except shoulder stretch).
- The PACER (16 m or 20 m), one-mile run/walk, and shoulder stretch may be administered to small groups of subjects at once. However, it may be necessary or most appropriate to provide partners for assistance.
- The following items can be administered to groups of two or three: dumbbell press, isometric push-up, push-up. Spotters should be provided for the dumbbell press.

SAFETY GUIDELINES AND PRECAUTIONS

Test items used in connection with the BPFT (including nontraditional ones) are typical of those used elsewhere in physical education or physical fitness programs. Some have appeared on disability-specific tests of physical fitness or tests classifying athletes with disabilities or are associated with ADLs. Although the BPFT is considered to be safe, the possibility that accidents may occur from activity must be recognized. The following guidelines and precautions should be followed when administering test items. It is also important to adhere to guidelines for specific test items presented later in this chapter and to other recommended professional practices.

- Personnel who administer the test should be qualified and knowledgeable about physical fitness testing and disability.
- Maximize the safety of all youngsters. Professionals using this test should follow the policies of their school or agency regarding medical information, medical records, and medical clearance for activity. Others should administer this test following approval by a physician who is aware of the health status of the youngster taking the test.
- Avoid administering tests under conditions of unusually high or low temperature or humidity or when windy. Youngsters with spinal cord injuries espe-

cially may be prone to problems with thermoregulation, including overheating.

- Be sure that youngsters understand test instructions. Provide opportunities for students to practice test items.
- Terminate the test item if youngsters experience dizziness, pain, or disorientation.
- Avoid comparison of performance among youngsters.
- Spot youngsters where necessary and appropriate.
- Incorporate warm-up and cool-down periods as appropriate for test items.
- Before testing have youngsters with spinal cord injuries above T6 empty their bowels and bladders and be checked for tight clothing, straps, or pressure sores that might contribute to skin irritation. Individuals with spinal injury above T6 are subject to autonomic dysreflexia, a condition that can dangerously elevate the heart rate and blood pressure as a result of bowel or bladder distension or skin irritation.
- Be aware that some heart rate monitors may use latex in the strap, which may cause allergic reactions. Wearing the strap thus may be contraindicated in certain instances.

AGE CONSIDERATIONS

For purposes of the BPFT the age of the individual is determined on the date the first test item is administered. Ages are not rounded to the nearest year. Thus, an individual who is 10 years and 11 months old should be identified as 10 years old.

AEROBIC FUNCTIONING

20-M PACER

In the 20-m PACER, participants run as long as possible back and forth across a 20-m (21.9 yd) distance at a specified pace, which gets faster each minute. The PACER is designed to measure aerobic capacity. The test is run on a flat, nonslippery surface. Participants run across the area to a line by the time that a beep from a tape sounds. At the sound of the beep, they turn around and run back to the other end. If a participant reaches the line before the beep, he or she must wait for the beep before running the other direction. Participants continue in this manner until they can no longer reach the line before the beep sounds. Participants not reaching the line when the beep sounds should be given two more beeps to regain the pace before they are withdrawn. In attempting to catch up, the entire 20-m lap must be completed. Participants who have completed the test should walk from the testing area to a designated cool-down area, being careful not to interfere with others who may still be running, and should continue to walk and stretch in the cool-down area.

Equipment

An audio cassette tape player with adequate volume, the PACER audio cassette, measuring tape, marker cones, pencil, and score sheets are required. Participants should wear shoes that prevent slipping. Plan for each participant to have a space 40 to 60 in. (100-150 cm) wide for running. The PACER tape has two musical versions and one with only beeps. Each version of the test gives a 5-s count-down then instructs participants to "begin." Cassette tapes are calibrated by using the 1-min test interval at the beginning of the tape. If the tape has stretched and timing is more than 5 s off, obtain another copy of the tape.

Scoring and Trials

One test trial is given. The individual's score is the number of completed laps.

Test Modifications

Runners who are blind may run with assistance of a partner, with guide wire or rope assistance, trailing along a wall, or using some other tactual assistance. The assisting partner can use a short tether rope, or runners who are blind can grasp the elbow of a sighted partner. After deciding the method of guidance, be sure it does not inhibit running performance. For validity, provide blind runners the opportunity to perform optimally. The runner should practice using the selected assistance until comfortable with it.

Be sure that youngsters with mental retardation understand how to perform the test. It is acceptable to take whatever time is necessary to ensure that participants learn the test. Because motivation is critical, at least one person should assume the responsibility of providing continual positive reinforcement to runners as they perform the test. Youngsters with mental retardation often need to run with a tester or aide. However, assistants must not pull or push runners or give any other physical advantage to the runner.

The 16-m PACER, which is discussed in the next test, is preferred for youngsters ages 10–12 or older with mental retardation if they exhibit low aerobic function-

AEROBIC FUNCTIONING

ing. As participants exhibit increased mastery, the test may be modified so that they run laps in one direction only around a track or running surface to enhance preparation for long-distance running.

Suggestions for Test Administration

- Mark the 20-m distance with marker cones and a tape or chalk line at each end.
- Before test day, participants should be allowed at least two practice sessions. Allow participants to listen to several minutes of the tape before they perform the test so that they know what to expect.
- The test tape contains 21 levels (21 min). The tape allows 9 s to run the distance during the first minute. The pace increases by approximately 1/2 second each following minute.
- Single beeps indicate the end of a lap. Triple beeps at the end of each minute indicate an increase in speed. Participants should be alerted that the speed will increase. Caution participants not to begin too fast: the beginning speed is very slow.
- If a participant cannot reach the line when the beep sounds, he or she should be given two beeps to attempt to regain the pace before being withdrawn. If the participant regains the pace, continue to count laps. Give credit for a lap only if the entire 20-m distance is completed.
- Volunteers can assist in recording scores.
- A whistle corresponding to beeps on the tape can be used if participants are unable to hear beeps from the cassette.

16-M PACER

The 16-m PACER is conducted as previously described, except the distance to be run is 16 m (17.5 yd) rather than 20 m. This shorter version is recommended particularly for youngsters with mental retardation and mild limitations in physical fitness.

TARGET AEROBIC MOVEMENT TEST

The TAMT is a modification of the aerobic movement test developed by Pat Good at Howe School, Dearborn, Michigan. This test measures the aerobic behavior of youngsters and the ability of youngsters to exercise at or above a recommended target heart rate (THR) for 15 min. Level 1, the basic level of the test, estimates the ability to sustain a moderate intensity of physical activity (i.e., 70% of maximal predicted heart rate) without exceeding 85% maximal predicted heart rate. Participants can engage in virtually any physical activity as long as the activity is of sufficient intensity to reach a minimal target heart rate (THR) and to sustain heart rate in a target heart rate zone (THRZ). In preparation for this test, testers are encouraged to work with youngsters to help them identify an appropriate physical activity.

For most participants—those who engage in whole-body forms of exercise (figure 5.1)—the THRZ is defined as 70% to 85% of a maximal predicted heart rate

AEROBIC FUNCTIONING

(operationally 140 to 180 beats/min). There are two exceptions to these general THRZ values. The first is for participants who have a spinal cord injury that results in low-level quadriplegia (LLQ, any spinal lesion between C6 and C8 inclusive). For these youngsters, THRZ may be defined in one of two ways. If a youngster has a resting (sitting) heart rate of less than 65 beats/min, the THRZ is defined as 85 to 100 beats/min. If a youngster's resting heart rate is 65 beats/min or more, the THRZ is defined as a range of 20 to 30 beats above the resting value. As an example, if a youngster has a resting heart rate of 75 beats/min, the THRZ will be 95 to 105 beats/min. The second exception applies to those who engage in strictly arm exercise (figure 5.2). For those who use arms-only forms of exercise, the THRZ is 130 to 170 beats/min. The tester checks the participant's heart rate at least once every 60 s. If participants are within their THRZ and no more than 10 beats above THR, the tester reinforces the behavior and encourages participants to continue at their present intensity of exercise (e.g., "Nice job! Just keep doing what you have been doing at the same speed."). If participants are below their THRZ, the tester encourages the participants to increase their exercise intensity (e.g., "Okay, your heart rate is a little low right now, so try to exercise a little harder or a little faster."). Should participants fall below their THRZ, they have 1 min to regain their minimal value. If they do, the test continues; if not, the test is terminated at that time. If the participant is above the THRZ or more than 10 beats over the THR, the tester should acknowledge the participant's effort but also encourage the participant to decrease exercise intensity (e.g., "Wow, you're really

Figure 5.1 Performing the target aerobic movement test.

AEROBIC FUNCTIONING

Figure 5.2 Performing the target aerobic movement test using arm ergometry.

working hard, in fact a little too hard! Try to exercise a little lighter or a little slower."). If participants work above their THRZ but complete the 15-min test, their results can be considered as meeting the criterion as long as they do not go below the THRZ requirements. If participants are beyond their THRZ for two or more consecutive minutes and they fail to reach the 15-min criterion, they should be retested at a later time and encouraged to work at a lower intensity for the purposes of the test.

Equipment

An exercise area large enough for adequate aerobic movement is necessary. An electronic heart rate monitor is recommended for administering this test. If a heart rate monitor is not available, a modified procedure using a stopwatch (or wristwatch that displays seconds) is optional. Music with a fast tempo is also recommended during the test to provide motivation and encourage rhythmic, steady-state exercise. Tape, CD, or record players are therefore optional.

Scoring and Trials

One test trial is given. This is a pass/fail test item; participants who can stay within or above the THRZ for 15 min pass the test. The 15-min count does not begin until

AEROBIC FUNCTIONING

after the participant enters the THRZ. For those unable to pass the test, it is recommended that testers note the length of time that the participant was able to exercise in the THRZ.

Test Modifications

If a heart rate monitor is unavailable, the test may be administered using the following procedures. The pulse rate at the wrist (i.e., radial pulse) is counted manually for 10-s intervals at a number of predetermined checkpoints. (The participant's exercise must be briefly interrupted for each pulse rate check.) The pulse rate is checked at the end of a 3-min warm-up period and at the end of each of the following exercise intervals after warm-up: 2 min, 4 min, 6 min, 9 min, 12 min, and 15 min. If youngsters are below the minimum THRZ value at any checkpoint, they should be encouraged to increase the intensity of their exercise and continue the test. If a youngster is below the THRZ for two consecutive checkpoints, however, the test is terminated. Youngsters should be encouraged to maintain a steady exercise pace rather than to fluctuate the exercise intensity. Minimal 10-s THRZ values and maximal THR values appear in table 5.1. It is recommended that the test be terminated if youngsters attain the maximal values during warm-up or test periods.

Table 5.1 Minimum and Maximum 10-s Heart Rate Values

	Minimum	Maximum
General	23	30
Quadriplegic (C6-C8)		
Resting HR < 65	14	17
Resting HR ≥ 65	(Resting HR + 20)/6	(Resting HR + 30)/6
Arm-only exercise (paraplegic)	22	28

Participants who are able to exercise within these 10-s pulse rate values for 15 min (following a 3-min warm-up) pass the test. If a youngster cannot pass the test, the tester should note the approximate length of time for which the youngster was in the THRZ based on the checkpoints. If a youngster is below or above the THRZ at one checkpoint but regains the THRZ at the next checkpoint, the youngster is credited for both checkpoints and the test continues. If participants work above their THRZ but complete the 15-min test, their results can be considered as meeting the criterion as long as they do not go below the THRZ requirements. If a youngster is below the THRZ for two consecutive checkpoints, however, the test ends, the participant is not credited for either checkpoint, and his or her score reverts back to the last checkpoint within the THRZ.

The TAMT can also be used to measure the ability to sustain more vigorous physical activity. However, it is not recommended that higher-level intensities be used for people with quadriplegia. Table 5.2 summarizes THR and THRZ information by levels.

AEROBIC FUNCTIONING

Table 5.2   Minimum Target Heart Rates and Target Heart Rate Zones for TAMT Levels

Prescribed level of intensity	Minimum predicted heart rate intensity	Minimum THR and THRZ for whole-body activity	Minimum THR and THRZ for arms-only activity
1 Moderate	70%	140 140-180	130 130-170
2 Low-level vigorous	75%	150 150-180	140 140-170
3 Vigorous	80%	160 160-180	150 150-170

Suggestions for Test Administration

- Provide a cool-down area and activities of decreasing intensity for participants at the conclusion of the test.
- In many cases it will be necessary to lead up to the test by discussing the procedures with participants and providing training sessions of shorter durations than required by the test. One method would be to start with a 5-min training session and periodically increase the duration by 3-min intervals until the participants are ready for the full exercise period.
- Individuals with spinal injuries above T6 are subject to autonomic dysreflexia, a condition that can elevate the heart rate and blood pressure as a result of bowel or bladder distension or skin irritation. As a precaution, therefore, it is recommended that youngsters with spinal cord injuries above T6 empty their bowels and bladders before testing and be checked for tight clothing, straps, or pressure sores that might contribute to skin irritation.
- Some participants require braces, such as thoracolumbosacral orthoses (TLSO braces), during testing. Medical personnel need to be consulted to determine whether participation in the specific physical activity is permitted and whether the brace needs to be worn. If a brace is worn, care must be taken to develop an acceptable method for securing a heart rate monitor. For example, in certain instances it may be possible to loosen the back brace, place the transmitter under the brace, and then tighten the brace to keep the transmitter in place. If it is not possible to use transmitters, the test modification using manual pulse rate counting may be required.

ONE-MILE RUN/WALK

In this test participants run or walk one mile (1,760 yd or 1,609 m) in the shortest time possible. The one-mile run/walk is used to measure aerobic capacity. Participants should be instructed to run or walk one mile at the fastest pace possible. The one-mile run/walk can be conducted on a track or any other flat, measured

AEROBIC FUNCTIONING

area. Examples of appropriately measured areas include a regulation track or a measured rectangle of 35 × 75 yd (32 × 68.6 m; 8 laps = 1 mile). Outside fields, playground areas, indoor court areas, or other grassy areas can be measured and marked to serve as an appropriate testing area.

Equipment

Stopwatch, scorecards, pencils, and clipboard are required.

Scoring and Trials

The one-mile run/walk is scored in minutes and seconds. One test trial is given.

Test Modifications

Runners who are blind may run with the assistance of a partner. Assistance can include a short tether rope, touching or grasping the elbow of a sighted partner, or running alongside a sighted partner who gives verbal direction and encouragement (figure 5.3, a–c). Once the method of ambulation is determined, it is important to ensure that it does not inhibit running performance. For purposes of validity, a runner who is blind must be given the opportunity to perform optimally. The runner should practice using the selected method of assistance until he or she is comfortable with it.

a   b   c

Figure 5.3 Performing the one-mile run/walk (*a*) with a sighted guide, (*b*) alone, and (*c*) with guide-rope assistance.

AEROBIC FUNCTIONING ▌▐

Suggestions for Test Administration

- Before the day of testing, provide practice as necessary for the required distance.
- After test completion, provide participants the opportunity to cool down by walking for several minutes.
- Participants should warm up properly before walking or running vigorously.
- Warm-up should include stretching exercises.
- It is recommended that youngsters not be tested in environments where the temperature plus the humidity is excessive.

BODY COMPOSITION

SKINFOLDS

This test determines the thickness of skinfolds at selected sites. Skinfold tests are used to estimate the body fat of youngsters. Skinfold measurements may be taken at three sites: triceps, subscapular, or calf. The triceps skinfold is taken over the triceps muscle at a location midway between the tip of the shoulder and the elbow (figure 5.4a). The subscapular skinfold is taken at a site approximately 1 in. (2.5 cm) below the tip of the scapula (inferior angle) and 1 in. (2.5 cm) toward the midline of the body (figure 5.4b). The calf skinfold is taken on the inside of the leg at about the level of maximal calf girth (figure 5.4c). The foot should be placed flat on an elevated surface with the knee flexed at a 90° angle. These measures should be taken on the participant's dominant or preferred side. Once the sites have been

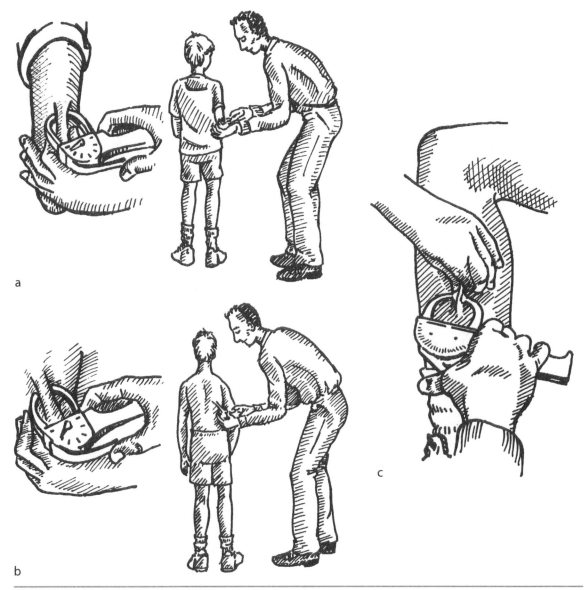

a

b

c

Figure 5.4 Skinfold measurements: (*a*) triceps, (*b*) subscapular, and (*c*) calf.

BODY COMPOSITION

identified, this is the recommended testing procedure: (1) Grasp the skinfold firmly between the thumb and forefinger and pull slightly from the body, being careful to include only subcutaneous fat tissue, not muscle, in the fold (the triceps and calf skinfolds are vertical folds, while the subscapular skinfold is an oblique fold; figure 5.4); (2) place the tips of the caliper slightly above or below (0.5 in. or 1.3 cm) the fingers grasping the skinfold; (3) slowly remove thumb pressure from the caliper, allowing it to exert full pressure on the fold; (4) record the thickness of the fold to the nearest millimeter once the needle settles (1 to 2 s); and (5) open the caliper completely before removing it so as not to pinch the participant.

Equipment

A skinfold caliper of good quality should be used to obtain skinfold measurements (figure 5.5). The instrument should provide a constant pressure of 10 g/mm^2 on the skinfold.

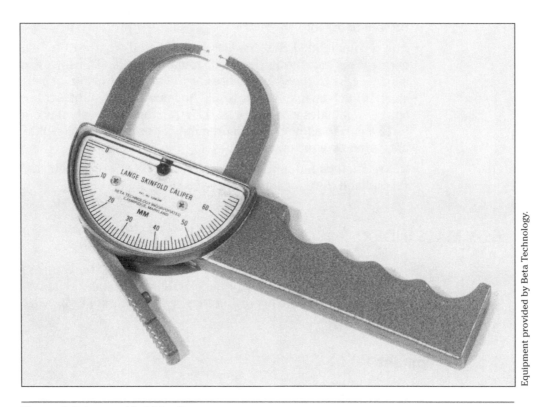

Equipment provided by Beta Technology.

Figure 5.5 Lange skinfold caliper.

Scoring and Trials

Three measurements should be taken at each skinfold site used. The median (middle) score should be the criterion score. If a skinfold reading at the same site differs from other readings by 2 mm or more, an additional measurement should be taken, and the measurement that is substantially different should be deleted.

BODY COMPOSITION

Test Modifications

Measurements should not be taken at sites with scar tissue, at sites where subdural or intramuscular injections have been received repeatedly, or on limbs that have muscular atrophy. In certain instances it may not be possible to attain skinfold measurements at a site.

Suggestions for Test Administration

- Testers should master administering the skinfold test before using the test.
- Testers can help distinguish muscle and fat by having participants tense and relax the triceps muscle.
- The subscapular skinfold is an oblique fold, in line with the natural cleavage lines of the skin. Testers may be aided in finding the line by having subjects bend their elbow and place the arm on the back so that the back of the hand touches the spine while standing. The top of the fold should be medial to the bottom of the fold.
- It is recommended that females being tested wear a thin T-shirt or similar garment for measuring the subscapular skinfold. The shirt can be raised to allow access to the skinfold sites or the measurement can be taken over the shirt. In such an instance, it would be necessary to subtract the fold of the T-shirt. For females wearing bras, the strap need be pushed upward only 2 to 3 in. (5-8 cm) to allow the measurement. If possible, female subjects should be measured by women.
- It is recommended that one measurement be taken at each site before taking second and third measurements at a site.

BODY MASS INDEX

Whereas skinfolds provide an estimate of body fatness, body mass index reflects fat, muscle and bone mass and provides an indication of the appropriateness of an individual's weight for his or her height. To compute BMI, height and weight must be determined.

Equipment

A scale is required, and a stadiometer is preferred. If a stadiometer is unavailable, a marked wall or tape measure can be used to determine height (or body length).

Scoring and Trials

Only one measurement of height and weight is necessary. Participants should wear lightweight clothing and remove shoes when possible for height and weight measurements. Initially, height can be rounded to the nearest 1/2 in. (1 cm) and

BODY COMPOSITION

weight to the nearest pound (1/2 kg). BMI can be determined by using the chart in appendix A or by using the following equations:

$$BMI = \text{Body weight (kg)/Height}^2 \text{ (m)}$$
$$BMI = \text{Body weight (lb.)} \times 704.5/\text{Height}^2\text{(in.)}$$

To convert to kilograms from pounds, divide total pounds by 2.2. To convert to meters from inches, divide total inches by 39.37. For example, the BMI of a 170-lb person who is 5 ft 10 in. (70 in.) tall is 24:

170 lb/2.2 = 77.3 kg	BMI = 170 (704.5)/(70)^2
70 in./39.37 = 1.78 m	= 119,765/4,900
BMI = 77.3/(1.78)^2 = 24	= 24

Test Modifications

The height of individuals who wear prosthetic devices or braces should be taken while they wear these devices. Subjects who are unable to support their body weight in a standing position can lie on a mat while body length is measured with a tape measure. If a youngster with cerebral palsy cannot stand erect because of exaggerated flexor tone in the hips or knees, the tester can use a tape measure to measure body segments (i.e., floor to knee, knee to hip, hip to head) and add the segments to determine body length for the purpose of calculating BMI.

The weight of individuals who wear prosthetic devices or braces is taken with braces and prosthetic devices removed or by subtracting the weight of the brace or prosthetic device. The weight of individuals who use wheelchairs can be determined either by taking the individual out of the wheelchair and weighing or by weighing the individual in the wheelchair and subtracting the weight of the wheelchair. Individuals with amputations and congenital anomalies can be weighed, but care must be taken when making comparisons with other people or calculating the BMI. When estimating the weight of a person with a leg amputation, add 1/18 of body weight for a below-knee amputation, 1/9 of body weight for an above-knee amputation, and 1/6 of body weight for a hip amputation.

Suggestions for Test Administration

This test may be waived if determination of either height or weight poses a safety problem to subject or tester; if anomalies, amputations, or contractures prohibit valid measurement; or if BMI will not be used for program planning.

MUSCULOSKELETAL FUNCTIONING: MUSCULAR STRENGTH AND ENDURANCE

BENCH PRESS

This test item and procedures for testing were modified from Johnson and Lavay (1989). In this test, participants attempt to perform as many bench presses as possible (to a maximum of 50 for males and 30 for females). This test is designed as a measure of upper extremity (particularly elbow extension) strength and endurance.

The participant lies supine on a bench with knees bent and feet on the floor or on rolled mats placed on each side of the bench. Individuals who are unable to assume this position should lie on the bench with knees flexed and lower extremities secured or supported. The tester acts as a spotter or has spotters for safety (figure 5.6). The participant grasps a 35-lb (15.9-kg) barbell with both hands directly above the shoulders and with elbows flexed; this is the ready position. Hands on the bar should be about shoulder-width apart with thumbs wrapped around the bar. On command the participant raises the barbell to a straight-arm position at a 90° angle to the body (figure 5.7) then returns to the ready position. The participant repeats this action without rest until the barbell cannot be raised any longer or until 50 repetitions for males or 30 repetitions for females have been successfully completed. One repetition should be completed every 3 to 4 s at a steady pace. Spotters stand beside and adjacent to the rib cage, rather than be-

Figure 5.6 Spotting and setting an upward target for the bench press.

MUSCULOSKELETAL FUNCTIONING: MUSCULAR STRENGTH AND ENDURANCE

Figure 5.7 The up position in the bench press.

hind the participant, so that the participant is encouraged to lift the barbell straight upward. Although a bilateral action with both arms is encouraged, participants are credited with a successful repetition if the barbell touches the chest and both arms eventually end up in a straight-arm position without rest. The tester encourages the participant through praise and counting of repetitions.

Equipment

Barbells and weights that together weigh 35 lb (15.9 kg) are required. A sturdy bench is recommended.

Scoring and Trials

Bringing the barbell from the chest to the straight-arm position represents one correct bench press. Record the number of correct bench press repetitions performed. Participants stop when they can no longer lift the weight completely or when they complete the required number of correct repetitions (50 for males and 30 for females).

MUSCULOSKELETAL FUNCTIONING: MUSCULAR STRENGTH AND ENDURANCE

Test Modifications

Be certain that subjects with mental retardation and mild limitations in physical fitness understand how to perform the test. It is essential to take whatever time is necessary for the participant to learn the test.

Subjects should have the upper-body ability to perform the test. Provide those with lower-body disability safe and stable support while they assume the supine position on a bench. Participants can be held or secured as necessary and appropriate for stability.

Suggestions for Test Administration

- Conduct practice sessions with participants to help them understand the proper method for performing the bench press. Stress safety in a positive manner through demonstrations.

- Demonstrate and let participants experiment with the proper method of performing the bench press with a broomstick, the bar only, with the bar and lighter weights, then finally with the 35-lb barbell. At the same time, demonstrate and let participants experience the proper position for lying on the bench, proper hand position on the bar, proper leg and foot position, and correct arm movement. Setting an upward target will enhance proper upward movement of the bar (figure 5.7). Give positive reinforcement for properly executed positions and movements. Do not test a participant who does not understand how to complete a properly performed repetition of the bench press.

CURL-UP

In the curl-up test, participants complete as many curl-ups as possible, up to a maximum of 75, at a cadence of one curl every 3 s. This test is designed to measure abdominal strength and endurance. The participant starts by lying in a supine position on a mat. The knees are bent at an angle of approximately 140°, with the feet flat on the floor and the legs slightly apart. The arms are held straight, parallel to the trunk, with the palms facing down toward the mat and the fingers outstretched. The participant is positioned so that the top of a measuring strip 4.5 in. (11.4 cm) wide can be touched with the outstretched fingers (figure 5.8). From the starting position, the participant curls up slowly, sliding the fingers across and to the opposite side of the measuring strip (figure 5.9). The participant then returns to the starting position. The important factor is that participants move the fingertips 4.5 in. (11.4 cm) as part of the curl-up. The tester should call the cadence (about one curl every 3 s). The participant continues without pausing until the pace cannot be maintained or until 75 repetitions have been completed.

MUSCULOSKELETAL FUNCTIONING: MUSCULAR STRENGTH AND ENDURANCE

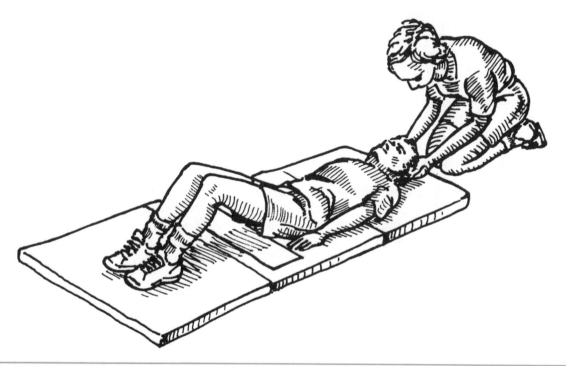

Figure 5.8 Starting position for the curl-up.

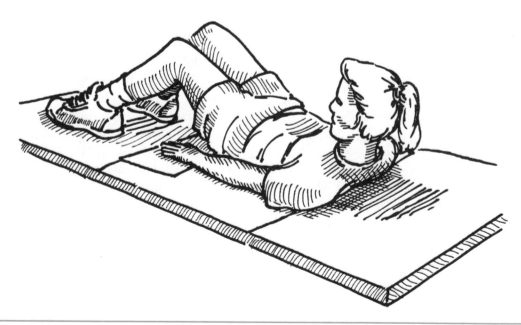

Figure 5.9 The up position for the curl-up.

MUSCULOSKELETAL FUNCTIONING: MUSCULAR STRENGTH AND ENDURANCE

Equipment

A gym mat and a measuring strip 30 in. × 4.5 in. (76 cm × 11.4 cm) are used in the test. The measuring strip can be held or secured to a supporting surface. Although measuring strips made from cardboard or sanded plywood are recommended, other systems for measuring the 4.5 in. are acceptable. For example, tape markers can be placed on a mat to indicate start and finish points.

Scoring and Trials

One trial is administered. An individual's score is the number of curl-ups performed correctly. One curl-up is counted for every return to a supine position on the mat. Curl-ups should not be counted if the feet completely leave the floor at any time during the movement or if the participant does not reach the required distance, does not return to the start position, or performs the curl-up in any other incorrect manner.

Test Modifications

It is acceptable to take whatever time is needed to ensure that youngsters know how to perform the test. Motivation is critical; therefore continual positive reinforcement should be provided throughout testing.

Suggestions for Test Administration

- Encourage a slow curling of the upper spine during the curl-up.
- Encourage steady, controlled, and continuous movement.
- It may be necessary for an assistant to secure the measuring strip.
- Time can be saved by taping a measuring strip to a large mat and adjusting the participant's starting position to the measuring strip.
- A testing assistant can cup his or her hands on the mat to guide the participant's head back to the appropriate down position on the mat (figure 5.8). Some youngsters are negatively affected by having their head contact an assistant's hands. This procedure can be eliminated if the participant is able to bring the head back gently on a suitably safe support surface.

MODIFIED CURL-UP

The modified curl-up is performed following the procedure recommended for the curl-up with the following exceptions:

- The hands are placed on the front of the thighs rather than on the mat alongside the body.

MUSCULOSKELETAL FUNCTIONING: MUSCULAR STRENGTH AND ENDURANCE

- As the participant curls up, the hands slide along the thighs until the fingertips contact the patellae (figure 5.10). (The hands should slide approximately 4 in. [10 cm], to the patellae or beyond, if necessary.)
- If necessary, testers can place their hands on the youngster's kneecaps to provide a more tangible target for the youngster's reach (figure 5.11).

Figure 5.10 Modified curl-up.

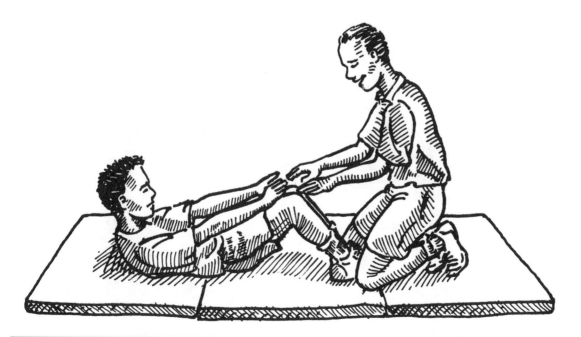

Figure 5.11 Setting a target for the modified curl-up.

MUSCULOSKELETAL FUNCTIONING: MUSCULAR STRENGTH AND ENDURANCE

DUMBBELL PRESS

In this test the participant lifts a 15-lb (6.8-kg) dumbbell as many times as possible, up to 50 repetitions, in a specific cadence. The test is designed to measure arm and shoulder strength and endurance. The participant is seated in a wheelchair or other sturdy chair (figure 5.12). The tester serves as a spotter or has spotters available for safety. The participant grasps the dumbbell with the dominant hand, with the elbow flexed so that the weight is close to and in front of the dominant shoulder. Once participants have control of the weight they should extend the elbow and flex the shoulder so that the weight is lifted straight up and above the shoulder. When the elbow is completely extended, the participant returns the weight to the starting position. The exercise is continued at a steady pace (approximately 3 to 4 s per repetition) until the participant is no longer able to lift the weight above the shoulder with complete elbow extension or until the participant completes 50 repetitions.

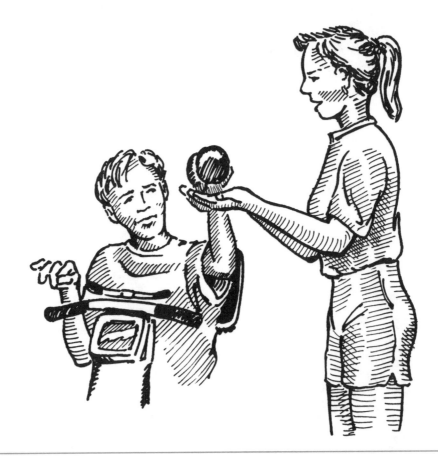

Figure 5.12 Dumbbell press.

MUSCULOSKELETAL FUNCTIONING: MUSCULAR STRENGTH AND ENDURANCE

Equipment

A 15-lb (6.8-kg) dumbbell, a stopwatch, and a wheelchair or other sturdy chair (preferably wood or metal) are required for this test.

Scoring and Trials

The participant receives one trial only. One successful lift is counted each time the dumbbell is raised above the shoulder with complete elbow extension. The scoring ends when the participant is unable to lift the weight with complete elbow extension, rests for more than 4 s between repetitions, or completes 50 repetitions.

Test Modifications

The test can be administered within the participant's range of motion. If complete elbow extension is not possible due to impairment, the tester should record a successful lift each time the participant lifts the weight with his or her maximal elbow range of motion.

During the test, a steady pace should be emphasized. If a participant requires more than 3 to 4 s to complete a repetition because of a disability, this should be permitted as long as the participant is working to lift the weight.

Suggestions for Test Administration

- Before testing, be sure the participant understands how to execute the movement.
- Provide continual encouragement throughout the test.
- Match counting with a cadence. For example, say "one and down, two and down, . . ." to a cadence of about one repetition every 3 to 4 s.

EXTENDED ARM HANG

In this test, the participant hangs from a bar or similar hanging apparatus for as long as possible, up to 40 s. The test is designed to measure hand, arm, and shoulder strength and endurance. The participant begins by grasping the bar using an overhand or pronated grip (knuckles toward the face; figure 5.13). The thumb should be wrapped around the bar. The participant may jump to this position, be lifted to it, or move to it from a chair. The participant must assume a fully extended position with feet clear off the floor throughout the test. Elbows and knees must not be bent. The participant can be steadied so that he or she does not sway.

MUSCULOSKELETAL FUNCTIONING: MUSCULAR STRENGTH AND ENDURANCE

Figure 5.13 Extended arm hang.

Equipment

This test item requires an adjustable bar about 1.5 in. (3.8 cm) in diameter at a height enabling performance without touching the support surface. The surface should be no more than 1 to 2 ft (30 to 62.5 cm) below the feet while the participant is in the hanging position. A gym mat should be placed under the bar. A stopwatch is required.

Scoring and Trials

One trial is permitted for each participant. The score is the elapsed time in seconds (to the nearest second) from the start of a free hang to the time that the fingers leave the bar.

MUSCULOSKELETAL FUNCTIONING: MUSCULAR STRENGTH AND ENDURANCE

Test Modifications

Individuals with disabilities must be provided an opportunity to learn and experience the test item before scores are recorded for testing purposes.

Suggestions for Test Administration

- Be sure that the bar and participant's hands are dry.
- Constant encouragement throughout the test is extremely important.
- Because some youngsters may be afraid of falling, it is important to keep them as close to the floor or ground as possible. Gently steady youngsters, and assure them that they will be assisted if they lose their grip.

FLEXED ARM HANG

In this test, the participant attempts to maintain a flexed arm position while hanging from a bar for as long as possible. The test is designed to measure hand, arm, and shoulder strength and endurance. The participant should grasp the bar with an overhand grip and be assisted to a position where the body is close to the bar and the chin is clearly over, but not touching, the bar. The participant attempts to hold this position for as long as possible. The body must not swing, the knees must not be bent, and the legs must not kick during the performance of the task. If a physical disability prohibits grasping, weight bearing, or reasonable execution, this item should not be administered.

Equipment

This test item requires a pull-up bar about 1.5 in. (3.8 cm) in diameter at a height exceeding the height of the participant, preferably no more than 3 ft (91 cm) and no less than 1.5 ft (46 cm) above the participant's standing height. A gym mat should be placed under the bar. A stopwatch is required.

Scoring and Trials

Each participant receives one trial. The tester records the length of time (to the nearest second) that the participant can maintain the flexed arm position. Timing stops when the head tilts back or the chin contacts or drops below the bar.

Suggestions for Test Administration

- A spotter can place an arm across the participant's thighs to restrict unwanted movements.

MUSCULOSKELETAL FUNCTIONING: MUSCULAR STRENGTH AND ENDURANCE

• Be sure participants understand how to perform the test before taking a score. Provide sufficient time for participants to learn the activity.

DOMINANT GRIP STRENGTH

In this test, participants attempt to squeeze a grip dynamometer with the stronger hand to generate as much force as possible. The test is designed to measure hand and arm strength. The participant should be seated on a straight-backed, armless chair, with feet flat on the floor. The tester must first adjust the handle of the dynamometer to fit the hand of the participant. When the dynamometer is squeezed, the second phalanx should rest on the adjustable handle. Once the dynamometer has been adjusted to the correct position, the participant should be instructed to squeeze the handle as hard as possible (figure 5.14). The hand grasping the dynamometer should be held away from the body and the chair while the test is performed.

Figure 5.14 Dominant grip strength.

MUSCULOSKELETAL FUNCTIONING: MUSCULAR STRENGTH AND ENDURANCE

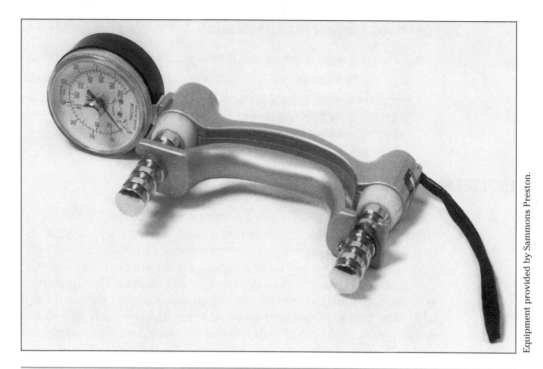

Equipment provided by Sammons Preston.

Figure 5.15 A grip dynamometer.

Equipment

A good quality grip dynamometer with an adjustable handle is recommended to conduct this test (figure 5.15). Data in the tables found in chapter 4 was collected using a JAMAR grip dynamometer.

Scoring and Trials

Three trials are administered. Allow at least 30 s between trials for each hand. The needle should be reset to zero after each trial. The tester records each participant's score to the nearest kilogram. The middle score of the three trials serves as the criterion score.

Test Modifications

The dominant grip strength test item should not be administered to individuals without sufficient functional strength or to those unable to grasp or release because of an impairment.

Participants can be seated in a wheelchair or on another support surface as long as the test can be administered appropriately.

MUSCULOSKELETAL FUNCTIONING: MUSCULAR STRENGTH AND ENDURANCE

Suggestions for Test Administration

- All participants must be motivated positively to enhance maximal effort.
- Do not test subjects until they have learned to perform the test properly.
- Individuals who are mentally retarded must be provided an opportunity to practice using the equipment and be taught the concept of squeezing as forcefully as possible.

ISOMETRIC PUSH-UP

This test item and procedures for testing were modified from Johnson and Lavay (1989). In the isometric push-up, participants attempt to hold a raised push-up position for up to 40 s. This test is designed primarily to measure the strength and endurance of the upper body. The participant assumes a front-leaning rest position with the hands directly below the shoulders, arms extended, the whole body in a straight line, and toes touching the floor or mat (the correct up position for a push-up; figure 5.16). The test is terminated when any movement—such as bending, sagging, or swaying—occurs at the elbows, shoulders, trunk, or knees. In other words, scoring is terminated when the correct up position for the push-up is no longer held.

Equipment

A stopwatch and a flat, solid surface are needed.

Scoring and Trials

One test trial is given. The tester records the length of time to the nearest second that the participant holds the proper position.

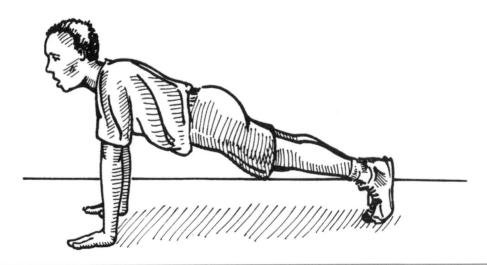

Figure 5.16 Isometric push-up.

MUSCULOSKELETAL FUNCTIONING: MUSCULAR STRENGTH AND ENDURANCE

Test Modifications

It is permissible to provide tactual assistance to help place and keep the body in the proper position during the test. However, no assistance should be given in holding the body upright.

Suggestions for Test Administration

- Do not test a participant who does not understand how to properly execute the isometric push-up.
- It is essential to take whatever time is necessary to ensure that participants learn the test.
- Since motivation is critical, it is important to provide continual positive reinforcement to each participant.
- Demonstrate and let participants experiment with the proper method of performing an isometric push-up, including the proper hand, arm, head, trunk, leg, and foot positions. Give visual, verbal, and physical support prompts to help participants learn the correct position. Physical supports during testing are not permitted.

PULL-UP

In this test, participants complete as many pull-ups as they can. The test is designed to measure upper-body strength and endurance. The participant begins from a straight-arm hanging position from a bar using an overhand (pronated) grip. The participant then pulls the body up toward the bar until the chin is above the bar (figure 5.17, a–b). Once this position is reached, the body is lowered to the full-hanging starting position. The body must not swing, the knees must not be bent, and the legs must not kick during the performance of the task.

Equipment

A sturdy horizontal bar about 1.5 in. (3.8 cm) in diameter that permits the participant to hang with arms fully extended and feet not touching the floor is used. A gym mat should be placed under the bar.

Scoring and Trials

Each participant is permitted one trial, and the score attained is the number of pull-ups performed. There is no time limit for the test, but participants should be encouraged to complete the test quickly to reduce the effects of fatigue.

Test Modifications

Testing assistants may need to spot participants to reduce the possibility of falling and losing balance.

MUSCULOSKELETAL FUNCTIONING: MUSCULAR STRENGTH AND ENDURANCE

Figure 5.17 Pull-up: (*a*) down position; (*b*) up position.

Suggestions for Test Administration

- Be sure participants understand how to perform the test before taking a score. Provide sufficient time for participants to learn to perform the test item with confidence.

- Spotters may place an arm across the participant's thighs to restrict swinging of the body, kicking, or other unwanted movements during the task.

MUSCULOSKELETAL FUNCTIONING: MUSCULAR STRENGTH AND ENDURANCE

MODIFIED PULL-UP

In this test, participants attempt to execute as many pull-ups as possible using a pull-up stand. The test is a measure of upper-body strength and endurance. A modified pull-up apparatus is used for the test (see appendix B and figures 5.18 and 5.19). The participant lies down under the crossbar, which is directly over the shoulders. The participant's arms are extended up toward the bar. The bar should be set 1 to 2 in. (3-5 cm) above the participant's outstretched arms. An elastic band is placed on a peg 7 to 8 in. (18-20 cm) below the bar. This band marks the height to which the participant's chin must rise for completion of one repetition.

Figure 5.18 Modified pull-up, starting position.

To get into the starting position, the participant raises the body high enough to grasp the bar, using an overhand grip (pronated) with thumbs around the bar. The pull-up begins in the down position, with arms, legs, and body straight; buttocks off the floor; and only the heels touching the floor.

MUSCULOSKELETAL FUNCTIONING: MUSCULAR STRENGTH AND ENDURANCE

Figure 5.19 Modified pull-up, raised position.

The pull-up action should raise the body to a height where the chin rises above the elastic band. Then the participant lowers to full extension and repeats as many times as possible. Movement is performed using the arms only.

Equipment

A modified pull-up stand is preferred. However, any adjustable bar arrangement can be used as long as procedures are followed.

Scoring and Trials

The number of correct pull-ups completed is the score. There is no time limit, but the action should be continuous.

Test Modifications

Participants with disabilities should be given sufficient practice to learn the test procedure.

MUSCULOSKELETAL FUNCTIONING: MUSCULAR STRENGTH AND ENDURANCE

Suggestions for Test Administration

- Encouragement and positive feedback should be given throughout the test.
- Stop the test if the participant experiences extreme discomfort.

PUSH-UP

In this test, participants complete as many push-ups as possible at a cadence of one push-up every 3 s. The test is designed primarily to measure upper-body strength and endurance. To begin, the participant assumes a prone position on a mat with hands placed under the shoulders, fingers outstretched, legs straight and slightly apart, and weight on tucked toes. The participant pushes to the up position until arms are straight. The participant lowers the body by bending the elbows to a 90° angle. The participant then returns to the straight-arm position.

Equipment

Only a mat is required. A watch with a second hand, a metronome, or a tape with the correct cadence is recommended to keep cadence. Cadence can also be called out.

Scoring and Trials

After learning the test, one trial is permitted. A participant's score is the number of correctly executed push-ups. The start of the push-up is the up position with arms straight. One push-up is counted each time the participant bends the arms and returns to the straight-arm position. The test is terminated if the participant is unable to maintain correct cadence, stops to rest, or discontinues the activity. Push-ups done incorrectly should not be counted. Incorrect push-ups occur if knees touch the floor, arms are not straight in the up position, arms are not bent to 90° on the downward movement, movement is jerky or not coordinated bilaterally, or the back is not kept reasonably straight.

Test Modifications

Time should be provided for participants with mental retardation to learn the test. Some latitude is recommended in performing to a cadence.

Considerable time is required to teach the test to individuals with visual disabilities if they have not already learned how to perform the push-up. Provide tactual or kinesthetic cues to help youngsters know correct arm positions and recognize a straight back during the push-up.

Suggestions for Test Administration

- Be sure all participants have time to learn to perform the test item correctly.

MUSCULOSKELETAL FUNCTIONING: MUSCULAR STRENGTH AND ENDURANCE

- Encourage participants to breathe as they perform the activity. Preferably, participants will exhale while rising to the up position.
- To enhance learning the push-up, have participants watch themselves in a mirror. This is especially important in learning to bend the elbows to 90° and keeping the back straight in the up position.
- Practice with a cadence.

40-M PUSH/WALK

Participants walk or push their wheelchairs a distance of 40 m (43 yd 27 in.) with a 5-m (5 yd 17 in.) start zone at a speed that is comfortable for them (figure 5.20). This test item is designed to measure whether participants have the strength and endurance to traverse a distance of 40 m without reaching a moderate level of exertion. This is not a dash nor a race, and testers should not emphasize high speed as a component of this test. Youngsters should be encouraged to travel at the speed that they usually use for mobility around the community. To pass the test, participants must be able to cover the 40-m distance in 60 s or less while keeping the heart rate below the criterion for moderate exercise intensity.

Figure 5.20 Performing the 40-m push/walk.

MUSCULOSKELETAL FUNCTIONING: MUSCULAR STRENGTH AND ENDURANCE

Equipment

A watch with a second hand or stopwatch is necessary for this test. The test should be conducted on a hard, flat, smooth surface. A starting line is placed 45 m (49 yd 8 in.) from a finish line and a timing line is placed 5 m (5 yd 17 in.) from the starting line (figure 5.21). There should be a safety zone of at least 5 m beyond the finish line.

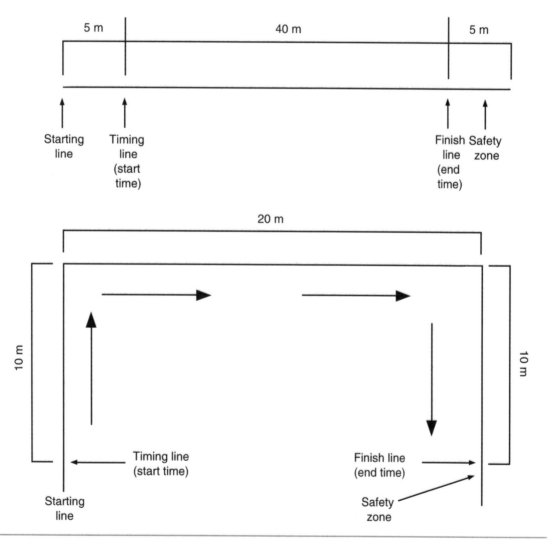

Figure 5.21 Acceptable courses for the 40-m push/walk.

Scoring and Trials

Participants are timed to the nearest second over the 40-m distance. The tester begins timing as the youngster crosses the timing line and stops timing when the youngster crosses the finish line. As soon as the participant crosses the finish line, the tester measures the participant's radial pulse for 10 s. For the correct

MUSCULOSKELETAL FUNCTIONING: MUSCULAR STRENGTH AND ENDURANCE

level of exercise intensity, participants who walk or push a wheelchair with their legs must have a posttest 10-s pulse rate of 20 beats or less. Youngsters who push a wheelchair with their arms must have a posttest 10-s pulse rate of 19 beats or less. Two trials can be administered, if necessary. If two trials are used, permit at least 1 min of rest between trials. The participant's pulse must be at or near resting level before a trial is administered. The test is assessed on a pass/fail basis. Participants pass when they cover the distance within 60 s at the acceptable heart rate intensity.

Test Modifications

If testers experience difficulty obtaining a radial pulse manually, it is recommended that they use a stethoscope to determine heart rate. Testers also can choose to use a heart rate monitor rather than taking a manual radial pulse. If a monitor is used, it should be read within 5 s after the youngster crosses the finish line. For youngsters who walk or push a wheelchair with their legs, the posttest heart rate on the monitor must be 125 beats/min or less. For participants who propel a chair with their arms, the rate must be 115 beats/min or less.

Suggestions for Test Administration

- If a youngster covers the distance in less than 60 s but the heart rate is too high, provide a rest, instruct the youngster to go slower, and retest.
- Testers should not use "on your mark, get set, go" or similar terminology to start the test. Instead, youngsters should start from the starting line when they are ready, and testers should begin timing as they cross the timing line.
- Testers can use youngsters' ratings of perceived exertion or tester observation of exertion to determine below-moderate effort in completing the test, although this procedure is not preferred because it is believed to be less accurate. For example, participants who are able to carry on a conversation comfortably or indicate that the activity was at a "light" exertion level might be considered to have exercised below a moderate level of intensity.

REVERSE CURL

For the reverse curl, the participant attempts to pick up a 1-lb (0.5-kg) dumbbell with the preferred arm while seated in a chair or wheelchair (figure 5.22). The test is designed as a measure of hand, wrist, and arm strength. During the movement, the fingers are flexed (i.e., wrapped around the weight), and the forearm is pronated at the start and throughout the movement. The movement is executed primarily by extending the wrist and flexing the elbow. It starts with the weight resting on the midpoint of the ipsilateral thigh while the participant is in a normal seated position. From this starting position, the participant flexes the elbow and lifts the weight until the elbow is flexed to at least 45°. The weight is held in this

MUSCULOSKELETAL FUNCTIONING: MUSCULAR STRENGTH AND ENDURANCE

Figure 5.22 Reverse curl.

position for 2 s and then is returned eccentrically to the starting position. The movement must be controlled, and the elbow extension on the downward movement must be slower than gravitational pull.

Equipment

A 1-lb (0.5-kg) soft-iron dumbbell is recommended.

Scoring and Trials

One trial is administered. Bringing the dumbbell from the thigh to the flexed arm position, holding it in the flexed position for 2 s, and returning it to the thigh represents one correct reverse curl. The test item is passed if the participant can perform one correct reverse curl.

Test Modifications

A table or other support surface can be used for a starting support surface in place of the thigh. If used, the support surface should be at the participant's knee level while seated.

Weights of 1 lb other than dumbbells can be used if the testing procedures can be essentially reproduced.

MUSCULOSKELETAL FUNCTIONING: MUSCULAR STRENGTH AND ENDURANCE

Suggestions for Test Administration

- Permit participants to practice the reverse curl before the formal test is administered.
- Provide a positive environment and positive reinforcement of good effort, proper execution, and successful completion of the task.

SEATED PUSH-UP

In this test, participants attempt to perform a seated push-up and hold it for up to 20 s. The test is designed to measure upper-body strength and endurance. Participants place their hands on the handles of the push-up blocks (figure 5.23), on the armrests of a wheelchair or an armchair and lift the body so that the buttocks are raised from the supporting surface by extension of the elbows. Once extension is obtained, participants attempt to maintain that position for as long as possible. Arms must be extended at the elbow.

Figure 5.23 Seated push-up.

MUSCULOSKELETAL FUNCTIONING: MUSCULAR STRENGTH AND ENDURANCE

Equipment

A stopwatch and either a standard wheelchair with armrests, a sturdy armchair, or a set of push-up blocks are required for the test. The armrests or push-up blocks should be slightly more than shoulder-width apart.

Scoring and Trials

The participant performs one trial only. The score is the length of time that the participant can hold the body off of the supporting surface or seat with elbow extension. Feet can come in contact with the floor but cannot be used to assist in performing the push-up. Timing begins when the participant raises the body and obtains elbow extension. Timing ends when the participant is no longer able to hold the position or after a maximum of 20 s.

Test Modifications

The test can be administered within the participant's range of motion as long as the buttocks are not in contact with the supporting surface. If the participant is unable to completely extend the elbows due to an impairment, timing should begin when the participant achieves his or her maximal extension and end when the maximal extension can no longer be held.

Suggestions for Test Administration

- Care must be taken to be sure that participants are in the correct position for testing.
- If using push-up blocks, the tester should stabilize the blocks before the test to prevent the blocks from tipping during the test.
- Give participants an opportunity to practice.

TRUNK LIFT

In this test item, the participant attempts to lift the upper body up to 12 in. (30 cm.) off the floor using muscles of the back and to hold the position to allow for measurement. The test is designed to measure trunk extension, strength, and flexibility. The participant lies on a mat in a prone position (face down). Toes are pointed, and hands are placed under the thighs. The participant lifts the upper body off the floor to a maximum height of 12 in. (figure 5.24). The movement should be performed in a very slow and controlled manner, with the bottom of the chin parallel to the floor. The position is held long enough to allow the tester to measure the distance from the participant's chin to the floor. The ruler should be placed on the floor at least 1 in. (2.5 cm) in front of the participant's chin, not

MUSCULOSKELETAL FUNCTIONING: MUSCULAR STRENGTH AND ENDURANCE

directly under the chin. After the tester makes the measurement, the participant returns to the starting position in a controlled manner.

Equipment

Gym mats and a yardstick or ruler are needed.

Scoring and Trials

Allow two trials, and record the better score. The score is recorded to the nearest inch (or nearest cm). Stretches above 12 in. (30 cm) are discouraged; distances above 12 in. (or 30 cm) therefore should be recorded as 12 in (or 30 cm).

Test Modifications

It is permissible to hold the legs of a person with mental retardation in place on the mat during the test.

Individuals with disabilities should be given sufficient time to practice the test and become thoroughly familiar with the testing procedure. When explaining the test item to subjects who are blind, it may be helpful to have them feel an individual demonstrating the skill.

Suggestions for Test Administration

- Do not allow participants to do ballistic (bouncing) movements.
- Do not encourage participants to rise higher than 12 in. (30 cm). Excessive arching of the back can cause compression of the disks.

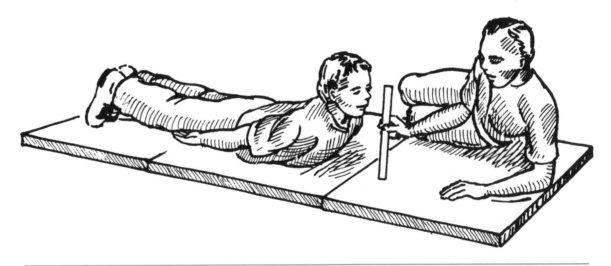

Figure 5.24 Trunk lift.

MUSCULOSKELETAL FUNCTIONING: MUSCULAR STRENGTH AND ENDURANCE

- Because motivation is an important factor, give positive reinforcement continually throughout the test.
- It is important to pay attention to performance technique during this test.

WHEELCHAIR RAMP TEST

Participants in wheelchairs attempt to push their chairs up a standard wheelchair ramp. This test item is designed to measure upper body strength and endurance. The participants may use whatever wheelchair push technique they prefer to complete the test.

Equipment

A standard wheelchair ramp is required. A standard ramp is one that complies with the American National Standards Institute (ANSI) guidelines, which specify that ramps should be at least 36 in. (91 cm) wide and constructed with 12 in. (30 cm) of run for every inch (2.5 cm) of rise (e.g., if the ramp has an elevation of 14 in., the length of the ramp should be 14 ft). For this test the ramp must be at least 8 ft (2.4 m) long (i.e., 8 ft of run) but need not be longer than 30 ft (9.1 m). On longer ramps, testers should place lines 8 ft (2.4 m), 15 ft (4.6 m), and 30 ft (9.1 m) from the start of the incline. (Ramps longer than 30 ft generally have a level platform at the 30-ft mark.) It is anticipated that testers will use ramps that already exist in their schools or buildings to conduct this test, although a ramp with sufficient run is not difficult to construct (see appendix B).

Scoring and Trials

Participants start with their lead wheels off the ramp and attempt to get their rear wheels beyond the lines on the ramp. Going beyond the 8-ft (2.4-m) line satisfies the minimal standard for this test. The preferred standard is obtained when the youngster either goes beyond the 15-ft (4.6-m) line or makes it to the top of a longer ramp that the youngster frequently encounters (e.g., a 20-ft ramp that leads to the entrance of the school). Testers therefore can set a preferred standard between 15 and 30 ft (4.6 and 9.1 m) based on the environment that a youngster must negotiate. The test is not timed, and multiple trials are permissible as appropriate.

Test Modifications

The test can be conducted on a ramp that does not meet the ANSI incline standards, provided that it is otherwise safe, but the tester will have to develop individualized standards.

Suggestions for Test Administration

Safety precautions should be taken to ensure that the wheelchair cannot roll off the edge of the ramp. Participants should be spotted from behind in case the wheelchair begins to roll back down the incline.

MUSCULOSKELETAL FUNCTIONING: FLEXIBILITY OR RANGE OF MOTION

MODIFIED APLEY TEST

The participant attempts to reach back and touch with one hand the superior medial angle of the opposite scapula (figure 5.25). The test is designed to measure upper-body flexibility.

Equipment

None.

Scoring and Trials

One trial is given for each arm. If the participant can successfully touch the superior medial angle of the opposite scapula and hold that position for 1 to 2 s, a score of 3 is awarded for that arm. If the participant cannot achieve a score of 3, he or she attempts to touch the top of the head. A successful attempt obtains a score of 2. If the participant cannot achieve a score of 2, he or she attempts to touch the mouth and receives a score of 1 if successful. If the participant is unable to touch the mouth, a score of 0 is given for that arm. The scoring scheme is summarized as follows (figure 5.26, a–c):

3—Touch the superior medial angle of opposite scapula

2—Touch the top of the head

1—Touch the mouth

0—Unable to touch the mouth

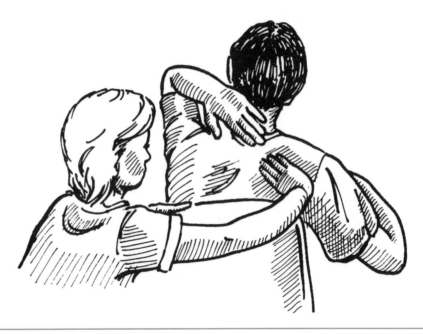

Figure 5.25 Administering the modified Apley test.

MUSCULOSKELETAL FUNCTIONING: FLEXIBILITY OR RANGE OF MOTION

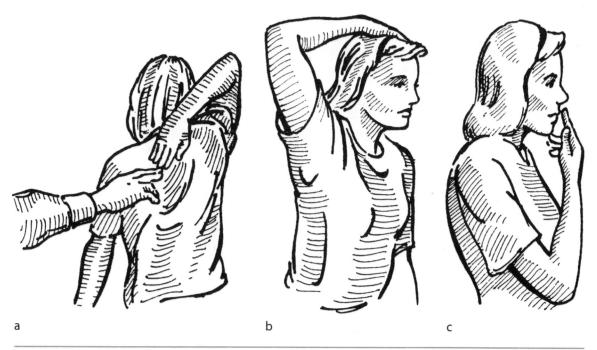

a   b   c

Figure 5.26 Scoring the modified Apley test: (*a*) scapula, score of 3; (*b*) top of head, score of 2; (*c*) mouth, score of 1.

Test Modifications

None.

Suggestions for Test Administration

- Testers can place their fingertips along the superior medial angle of the scapula (or on the top of the head) to provide a target for the participant and a more objective criterion for scoring (i.e., if the participant can touch the tester's fingertips, a passing score is awarded).
- Participants should be given ample opportunity to practice this test. Physical assistance may be provided during practice but not during the test.
- Participants should be given encouragement and positive reinforcement.
- Testers must require youngsters to hold the test position briefly (1-2 s) to award a score of 3. Ballistic or reflexive touches are not acceptable.
- Sufficient warm-up including shoulder-stretching activities should precede testing.

BACK-SAVER SIT AND REACH

The object of this test is to reach across a sit-and-reach box while keeping one leg straight. The test item is designed to measure flexibility of the hamstring muscles.

MUSCULOSKELETAL FUNCTIONING: FLEXIBILITY OR RANGE OF MOTION

The participant begins the test by removing his or her shoes (very thin footwear is permitted) and sitting down at the test apparatus. One leg is fully extended with the foot flat against the end of the testing instrument. The other knee is bent, with the sole of the foot flat on the floor 2 to 3 in. (5-8 cm) to the side of the straight knee. The arms are extended forward over the measuring scale with the hands palms down, one on top of the other. The participant reaches directly forward with both hands along the scale four times and holds the position of the fourth reach for at least 1 s (figure 5.27, a–b). After measuring one side, the participant switches the position of the legs and reaches again. The participant can allow the bent knee to move to the side if necessary as the body moves by it.

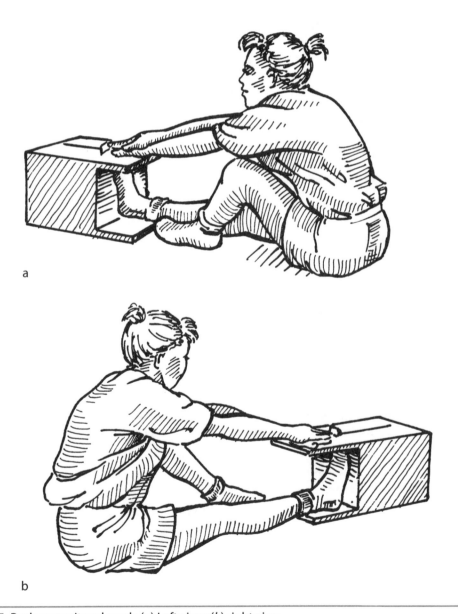

a

b

Figure 5.27 Back-saver sit and reach. (*a*) Left view; (*b*) right view.

MUSCULOSKELETAL FUNCTIONING: FLEXIBILITY OR RANGE OF MOTION

Equipment

This measurement is best taken using a flexibility testing apparatus approximately 12 in. (30 cm) high and 12 in. wide. A measuring scale is placed on top of the apparatus with the zero end of the ruler nearest the participant and the 9-in. (23-cm) mark even with the vertical surface against which the foot rests (see appendix B and figures 5.27, a–b and 5.28). The grid on the box should range from 0 to at least 16 in. (40 cm).

Figure 5.28 A commercially built Flex-Tester.

Scoring and Trials

One trial (four stretches, holding the last) for each leg is given for this test. The tester records to the nearest whole unit the number of inches or centimeters reached in the last attempt on each side. Reaches beyond the criterion-referenced standards designated for this test item are not recommended.

Test Modifications

Subjects with mental retardation should be given sufficient practice time to become completely familiar with the testing procedure. They should not be encouraged to exceed the recommended criterion-referenced standards for this test item.

MUSCULOSKELETAL FUNCTIONING: FLEXIBILITY OR RANGE OF MOTION

Verbal description of the testing environment and procedure is necessary for blind subjects. They may be given physical assistance as they practice the test and become familiar with the procedure. Physical assistance may not be given during the test itself, however.

If a flexibility testing apparatus is not available, a ruler extended over a bench turned on its side may be used to obtain measurements. This may be less accurate than the recommended testing apparatus.

Suggestions for Test Administration

- The knee of the extended leg must remain straight. The tester should place one hand on the straightened leg to assist proper positioning.
- The participant's hands should reach forward evenly, and the shoulders should be square to the test apparatus.
- Hips must remain square to the box. Do not allow participants to turn their hip away from the box as they reach.
- Require participants to stretch the hamstrings and lower back as a warm-up before testing.
- Because motivation is an important factor, participants should receive continual encouragement and positive reinforcement during the testing process.
- Emphasize a gradual reach forward. Bobbing or jerking movements forward should not be permitted.

SHOULDER STRETCH

This test item is used to determine whether a participant is able to touch the fingertips together behind the back by reaching over the shoulder and down the back with one arm and across the back with the other arm (figure 5.29). This test item measures upper-body flexibility. The measure is designated *right* or *left* on the basis of the arm reaching over the shoulder. Thus when the right arm stretches over the right shoulder, it is a right-arm stretch.

Equipment

None.

Scoring and Trials

One test trial is permitted. The test is scored on a pass/fail basis. The participant passes if the fingers touch and fails if the fingers do not touch.

Test Modifications

Physical assistance and verbal direction may be given to participants as they practice the test. Physical assistance may not be given during the test itself, however.

MUSCULOSKELETAL FUNCTIONING: FLEXIBILITY OR RANGE OF MOTION

Figure 5.29 Shoulder stretch: right shoulder.

Suggestions for Test Administration

- The participants should be given ample opportunity to practice this testing procedure.
- Upper-body stretching, including approximations of the test itself, is recommended as a warm-up.

MODIFIED THOMAS TEST

The test is designed to assess the length of the participant's hip flexor muscles. The test is conducted on a sturdy table (figures 5.30 and 5.31, a–b). The tester places a thin strip of masking tape on the table 11 in. (28 cm) from one of the short edges. The participant lies in a supine position on the table so that the head of the femur is level with the strip of tape. (The tester should ensure that the hip joint is 11 in. from the edge of the table.) The lower legs can be relaxed and should hang off the narrow edge of the table. To test the right hip, the participant lifts the left knee toward the chest. The participant uses the hands to pull the knee toward the chest until the back is flat against the table. At that point, the tester should observe the position of the participant's right thigh. Participants receive the

MUSCULOSKELETAL FUNCTIONING: FLEXIBILITY OR RANGE OF MOTION

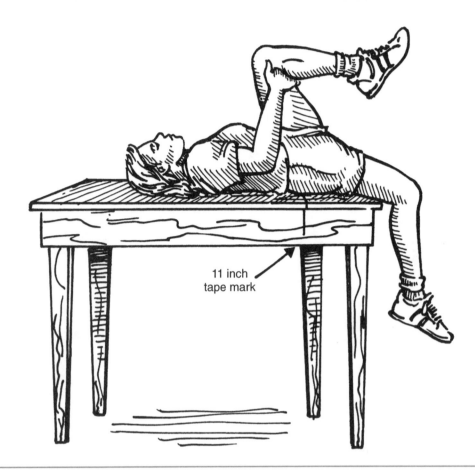

11 inch tape mark

Figure 5.30 Modified Thomas test: score of 3.

maximum score if they can keep the thigh in contact with the table surface while the back is flat. To test the left hip, the procedure is repeated on the opposite side of the body.

Equipment

A sturdy table with a tape mark 11 in. (28 cm) from one of the short edges of the table is required. A 3 × 5 in. (7.6 cm tall) file card and a 4 × 6 in. (15.2 cm wide) file card or equivalents are recommended to help with the scoring. A tape measure or a ruler can also be used.

Scoring and Trials

One trial for each leg is appropriate for most participants. The test is scored on a scale of 0 to 3 points as follows:

3—The tested leg remains in contact with the surface of the table when the opposite knee is pulled toward the chest, and the back is flat (figure 5.30).

MUSCULOSKELETAL FUNCTIONING: FLEXIBILITY OR RANGE OF MOTION

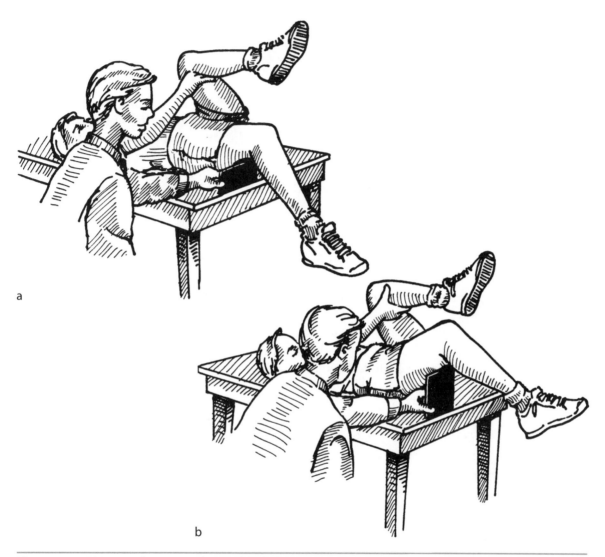

Figure 5.31 Using cards to score the modified Thomas test: (*a*) score of 1; (*b*) score of 0.

2—The tested leg does not remain in contact with the surface of the table, but the height of the participant's leg above the edge of the table is less than 3 in. or 7.6 cm (e.g., if the leg is elevated but the tester cannot slide the 3-in. [7.6-cm] side of the small file card under the participant's leg at the edge of the table, a score of 2 is appropriate).

1—The tested leg lifts more that 3 in. (7.6 cm) but less than 6 in. (15.2 cm) above the edge of the table (e.g., if the 3-in. [7.6-cm] side of the small file card slides under the participant's leg at the edge of the table, but the 6-in. [15.2-cm] side of the large card does not, a score of 1 is appropriate; figure 5.31a).

0—The tested leg lifts more than 6 in. (15.2 cm) above the edge of the table (e.g., if the 6-in. [15.2-cm] side of the large file card slides under the participant's leg at the edge of the table, a score of 0 is appropriate; figure 5.31b).

MUSCULOSKELETAL FUNCTIONING: FLEXIBILITY OR RANGE OF MOTION

Test Modifications

If necessary, a tester or spotter can gently assist the participant in pulling the opposite knee toward the chest. In any event, it is important that the back be flat on the table before scoring the test.

If a youngster is unable to flatten the lower back after multiple attempts, the tester should score the test as previously indicated and note on the score sheet that the back was not flat. Scores obtained in this manner should not be compared with the general or specific standards recommended in this manual. Instead, these scores can be used to monitor future progress, and testers are encouraged to develop individualized standards for the youngster.

Suggestions for Test Administration

- Participants should stretch or otherwise warm up the hip muscles before testing.
- If testers prefer to use a tape measure or ruler to evaluate the extent of elevation of the tested leg, the measurement should be taken vertically from the edge of the table to the posterior aspect of the upper leg.
- Testers can determine flatness of the participant's lower back by attempting to pass their hand between the hollow part of the lower back and the table. Ordinarily, the hand is unable to move between the lower back and the table if the back is flat.
- Testers should note any knee extension or thigh abduction that occurs during the test for youngsters who score a 3. If the rectus femoris extends the knee or the tensor fasciae latae abducts the thigh, this indicates that some of the hip flexors (iliopsoas and sartorius) are of normal length but that others may be shortened.

TARGET STRETCH TEST

The target stretch test (TST) is a screening instrument used to estimate movement extent in a joint. It includes a series of tests illustrated in the sketches in form 5.1. For each individual test, testers ask participants to achieve their maximal movement extent for a given joint action and subjectively evaluate that limit against criteria provided in the sketches. Testers should demonstrate or clearly describe the optimal (i.e., complete) movement extent for each joint being tested. Descriptions of individual items follow.

Wrist Extension

The participant's recommended test position is either standing or seated with the elbow flexed to 90° and the forearm pronated (palm down). Participants extend the wrist as far as possible, and testers read the angle made by the longitudinal axis (i.e., lengthwise middle) of the lateral aspect of the hand (not the fingers).

MUSCULOSKELETAL FUNCTIONING: FLEXIBILITY OR RANGE OF MOTION

Elbow Extension

The participant's recommended test position is either standing erect or seated with the upper arm at the side. Preferably, the forearm should be supinated (palm facing forward). Participants extend the elbow as far as possible, and testers read the angle made by the longitudinal axis of the forearm from elbow to wrist (not the hand or fingers).

Shoulder Extension

The participant's recommended test position is either standing erect or seated with the arm at the side (palm facing the side). Participants extend the shoulder backward in a vertical plane as far as possible, and testers read the angle made by the longitudinal axis of the upper arm from shoulder to elbow while ensuring that the participant's trunk remains erect.

Shoulder Abduction

The participant's recommended test position is either standing erect or seated with the arm at the side. Participants abduct the shoulder as far as possible, and testers read the angle made by the longitudinal axis of the upper arm from the shoulder to the elbow while ensuring that the participant's trunk remains erect. When the shoulder is fully abducted the palm should face inward, i.e., toward the midline of the body.

Shoulder External Rotation

The participant's recommended test position is seated so that the tester can evaluate the movement by observing the participant's shoulder from above. The recommended position also requires 90° of elbow flexion and contact between the upper arm and the lateral aspect of the trunk (i.e., adduction). Participants externally rotate the shoulder as far as possible by moving the wrist away from the trunk while maintaining an abducted upper arm and 90° of elbow flexion. The tester reads the angle made by the longitudinal axis of the forearm from elbow to wrist (figure 5.32).

Forearm Supination

The participant's recommended test position is either standing or seated facing the tester, with elbow flexed while holding a pencil (or similar object) in a closed fist. (The long end of the pencil should protrude up from the thumb side of the fist.) The participant supinates the forearm (palm up) as far as possible, and the tester reads the angle made by the long end of the pencil.

Forearm Pronation

The participant's recommended test position is either standing or seated facing the tester, with elbow flexed while holding a pencil (or similar object) in a closed fist. (The long end of the pencil should protrude up from the thumb side of the

MUSCULOSKELETAL FUNCTIONING: FLEXIBILITY OR RANGE OF MOTION

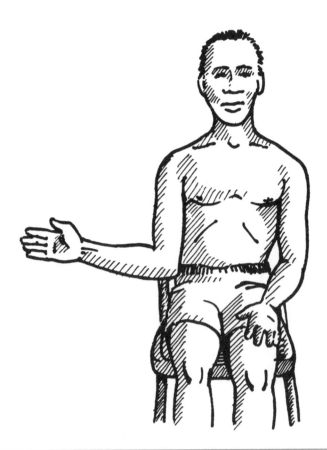

Figure 5.32 Position for right shoulder external rotation test.

fist.) The participant pronates the forearm (palm down) as far as possible, and the tester reads the angle made by the long end of the pencil.

Knee Extension

The recommended test position is to have the participant in a side-lying position on a rug or mat. (The bottom leg may be bent for stability while the top knee is being evaluated.) The tester views the extended leg from above while standing behind the knee being evaluated. The tester reads the angle made by the longitudinal axis of the lower leg from knee to ankle.

Equipment

No equipment is necessary for participants who are able to achieve the recommended test positions for each item. Testers compare the participant's movement to the criteria provided in the sketches. The test can be administered to participants who cannot achieve the recommended test position, but evaluation of performance may be enhanced by using a modified goniometer (figure 5.33). Use of this instrument is discussed under test modifications.

MUSCULOSKELETAL FUNCTIONING: FLEXIBILITY OR RANGE OF MOTION

Scoring and Trials

Participants must be able to hold their final position for at least 1 to 2 s. Using a TST worksheet (form 5.1), testers initially record the "time on the clock" (the degrees of an arc) of the movement extent to the nearest "half hour" (15°) and then convert the time to a test score (0-2) as given by the sketches. For example, a right wrist extension "time" of 1:00 receives a score of 2, and times between 1:30 and 2:00 receive a score of 1. Any time below 2:00 receives a score of 0. Noting time on the clock allows the tester to document changes in performance even if the test score does not change. The relationship between test scores and goniometric values is given in table 5.3.

Table 5.3   Goniometric Values Associated With Target Stretch Test Scores

	Normal[a]	2	1
Wrist extension	70°	60°	30°
Elbow extension	0°	0°	−15°
Shoulder extension	60°	60°	30°
Shoulder abduction	170°	165°	120°
Shoulder external rotation	90°	75°	30°
Supination/pronation	90°	90°	45°
Knee extension	0°	0°	−15°

[a] Normal, or typical, range-of-motion values found in the literature vary somewhat from authority to authority. These values come from Cole and Tobis (1990). In some cases, values for test scores of 2 differ from Cole's and Tobis's values due to the recommendation that testers estimate movement extent to the nearest "half hour" (15°). In the case of shoulder external rotation, some of the difference between a normal score and a score of 2 is due to differences in test procedures.

Test Modifications

If a participant cannot achieve the recommended test position depicted in the sketch, the joint action can still be assessed, but the clock must be rotated for scoring. For instance, the recommended test position for right wrist extension includes maintaining elbow flexion of 90°. A participant, however, could be tested with the arm at the side and a completely extended elbow if the clock is rotated 90° so that the 9 instead of the 12 is at the top of the clock. This may become conceptually difficult for the tester, so it is recommended that testers modify a transparent plastic goniometer to help rotate the clock into the proper position. The circular dial of the goniometer can be converted into a "clock face" by placing the numerals 1 to 12 on strips of tape at 30° intervals (figure 5.33a). Once the goniometer is modified, it can be used to rotate the clock and estimate movement extent from a variety of test positions. When using the modified goniometer, it is recommended that testers stand, crouch, or kneel approximately 5 to 10 ft (1.5-3 m)

MUSCULOSKELETAL FUNCTIONING: FLEXIBILITY OR RANGE OF MOTION

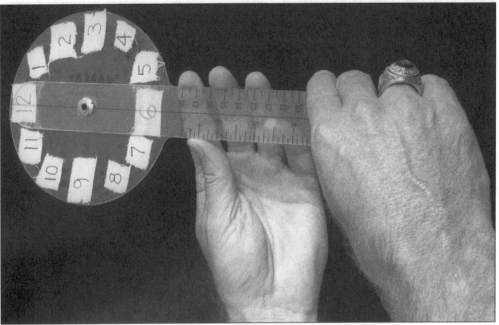

a

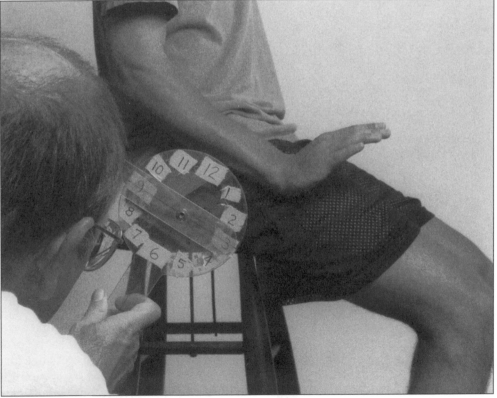

b

Equipment provided by Sammons Preston.

Figure 5.33 Modified goniometer: (*a*) close-up view; (*b*) measuring wrist extension.

MUSCULOSKELETAL FUNCTIONING: FLEXIBILITY OR RANGE OF MOTION

from the participant. The tester reads the time on the clock by holding the goniometer at arm's length and viewing the limb in question through the face of the goniometer (figure 5.33b).

Suggestions for Test Administration

- Testers should help participants maximize their movement extent. Changes in body position may influence a youngster's performance. Youngsters who have tonic neck reflexes, for instance, may enhance their performance by either flexing, extending, or turning the head while being tested. Testers should help youngsters find the position that maximizes the movement extent in a joint, as long as the position is noted on the worksheet and the integrity of the scoring system is maintained (i.e., the clock may need to be rotated).

- When evaluating a number of participants, testers can expedite the testing process by recording the movement extent on the clock during testing and converting it to a score after the testing session.

- Participants should warm up the joints to be tested.

- Testers may find it helpful to tape photocopies of the sketches (enlargements work best) to a nearby wall to eliminate flipping back and forth between pages in the manual or worksheet.

Testers who administer the TST might find the worksheet in form 5.1 helpful and are free to photocopy the form as often as necessary. The sketches demonstrate the recommended test positions, the clock for scoring, and the criteria for minimal (a score of 1) and preferred (a score of 2) standards. Spaces are available to the right of each sketch to record both time on the clock (degree of movement) to the nearest half hour and corresponding test score (0-2). After using the worksheet, testers can transfer test scores to the BPFT test form (form 3.1 on p. 36). Extra spaces are provided to allow multiple administrations of the test. Below each sketch is room to note any variation in test position that might be necessary when youngsters cannot attain the recommended test position. There is also room to note other relevant observations.

Form 5.1 Target Stretch Test

a) Wrist extension – right

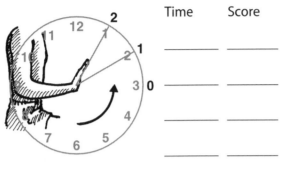

Time   Score

1 _____ _____

0 _____ _____

_____ _____

_____ _____

Position _____

Comments _____

b) Wrist extension – left

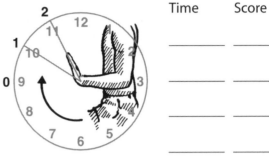

Time   Score

_____ _____

_____ _____

_____ _____

_____ _____

Position _____

Comments _____

c) Elbow extension – right

Time   Score

_____ _____

_____ _____

_____ _____

_____ _____

Position _____

Comments _____

d) Elbow extension – left

Time   Score

_____ _____

_____ _____

_____ _____

_____ _____

Position _____

Comments _____

e) Shoulder extension – right

Time   Score

_____ _____

_____ _____

_____ _____

_____ _____

Position _____

Comments _____

f) Shoulder extension – left

Time   Score

_____ _____

_____ _____

_____ _____

_____ _____

Position _____

Comments _____

Form 5.1

g) Shoulder abduction – right

Time	Score
_____	_____
_____	_____
_____	_____
_____	_____

Position _____

Comments _____

h) Shoulder abduction – left

Time	Score
_____	_____
_____	_____
_____	_____
_____	_____

Position _____

Comments _____

i) Shoulder external rotation – right

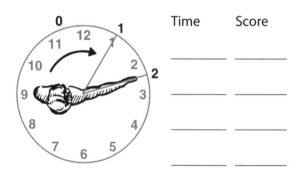

Time	Score
_____	_____
_____	_____
_____	_____
_____	_____

Position _____

Comments _____

j) Shoulder external rotation – left

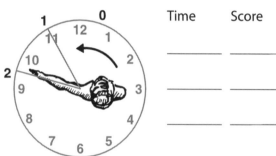

Time	Score
_____	_____
_____	_____
_____	_____
_____	_____

Position _____

Comments _____

k) Forearm supination – right

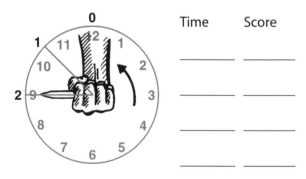

Time	Score
_____	_____
_____	_____
_____	_____
_____	_____

Position _____

Comments _____

l) Forearm supination – left

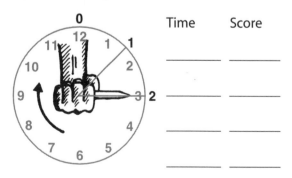

Time	Score
_____	_____
_____	_____
_____	_____
_____	_____

Position _____

Comments _____

(continued)

m) Forearm pronation – right

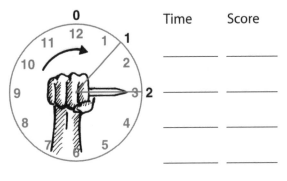

Time   Score

_____ _____

_____ _____

_____ _____

_____ _____

_____ _____

Position _____

Comments _____

n) Forearm pronation – left

Time   Score

_____ _____

_____ _____

_____ _____

_____ _____

_____ _____

Position _____

Comments _____

o) Knee extension – right

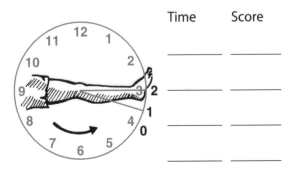

Time   Score

_____ _____

_____ _____

_____ _____

_____ _____

_____ _____

Position _____

Comments _____

p) Knee extension – left

Time   Score

_____ _____

_____ _____

_____ _____

_____ _____

_____ _____

Position _____

Comments _____

6

Testing Youngsters With Severe Disabilities

The Brockport Physical Fitness Test is appropriate for most youngsters with disabilities and unique needs related to physical fitness. However, it may be inappropriate for youngsters with severe disabilities for a variety of reasons. Often these reasons include the inability of such youngsters to perform field-based performance test items as described in the procedures presented in this manual. They may lack the levels of physical fitness, motivation, understanding, and basic motor ability required to perform test items. For such youngsters, two alternative orientations for assessment are offered in this chapter. These orientations may yield information about physical activity rather than physical fitness and may most appropriately be bases of individualized rather than health-related, criterion-referenced standards. However, their results may be helpful in designing programs that lead to acceptable levels of physical fitness or physical activity. The two orientations relate to task analysis and measurement of physical activity.

TASK ANALYSIS

A task analysis breaks movements, skills, or activities into tasks and subtasks. Tasks are associated with outcomes that can be targeted, learned, and measured. They represent points of focus in the performance of an activity. Ideally, they take a youngster from a present level of performance through activities leading to a terminal objective. There are a variety of ways to design a task analysis.

The use of task analysis for the development and assessment of physical fitness for people with severe disabilities is not new. Jansma, Decker, Ersing, McCubbin, and Combs (1988) presented the Project Transition Assessment System and contrasted it with the Data Based Gymnasium, the I CAN Adaptative Model, and Project

MOBILITEE assessment systems. All these programs use task analysis. These authors also summarized factors that require attention if a satisfactory assessment of individuals with severe disabilities is to be the result. In brief, these include the need for task-analytic procedures, more frequent data collection, unobtrusive informal observational measures, the use of verbal and nonverbal cues, age appropriateness, maintenance and generalization of status, appropriate prompting levels, and systematic rapport. It is recommended that those interested in physical fitness testing for people with severe disabilities consult the programs previously identified. The assessment process associated with Project Transition (Jansma et al., 1988) in developing a task-analytic assessment system is also worth consideration.

The development of a task analysis is sometimes recommended in this manual for the purpose of leading youngsters toward acceptable levels of health-related, criterion-referenced levels of physical fitness. Table 6.1 presents one example of a task analysis using the isometric push-up test item of the BPFT. It is consistent with the process developed by Jansma et al. (1988) in connection with Project Transition.

MEASUREMENTS OF PHYSICAL ACTIVITY

Before we recommend procedures for measurement of physical activity, it is important to remember that physical activity and physical fitness are separate but related concepts. When measuring physical fitness, a characteristic or characteristics reflecting a set of attributes that people possess or achieve are measured (Caspersen et al., 1985; Freedson & Melanson, 1996). The BPFT is used to measure physical fitness. When measuring physical activity, a behavior reflecting energy expenditure is typically measured. Examples of physical activity measures that can be used include caloric expenditure; frequency, intensity, and duration of activity; and heart rate responses to exercise (Freedson & Melanson, 1996). These measurements can be attained or estimated using a variety of strategies, including direct observation, self-report measures, mechanical and electronic monitoring, and physiological measures. These strategies are presented and discussed in a variety of sources (Freedson & Melanson, 1996; Freedson, 1991). Pedometers, the Caltrac accelerometer, motion sensors, and heart rate monitors appear to hold promise for obtaining the most accurate measurements of physical activity for individuals with severe disabilities. Teachers are encouraged to monitor the frequency, intensity, and duration of the physical activity of youngsters with more severe involvement and to develop strategies for increasing those levels. Increases in physical activity often lead to increases in physical fitness, even if fitness cannot be validly assessed.

Because physical fitness and physical activity may have independent effects on health status (Blair et al., 1990), different standards may also be needed and recommended for each. The U.S. Centers for Disease Prevention and Control and the American College of Sports Medicine recommend 30 min or more of moderate-intensity physical activity on most, preferably all, days of the week and point out that additional health benefits can be attained through greater amounts of physical activity (Pate et al., 1995; President's Council on Physical Fitness and Sport, 1996). Because this manual focuses on physical fitness, standards relating to physical activity and health benefits are not discussed here. Suffice it to say that different standards for physical fitness and physical activity are appropriate.

Table 6.1 Task Analysis for an Isometric Push-Up

Objective: To execute an isometric push-up correctly for 3 s.

Directions: Circle the minimal level of assistance an individual requires when correctly performing a task. Total each column. Total the column scores, and enter the total score achieved in the summary section. Determine the percentage-of-independence score using the chart in the summary section. Record the amount of time the position is held for the product score.

Isometric push-up	IND	PPA	TPA
1. Lie face-down.	3	2	1
2. Place hands under shoulders.	3	2	1
3. Place legs straight, slightly apart, and parallel to the floor.	3	2	1
4. Tuck toes under feet.	3	2	1
5. Extend arms while body is in a straight line.	3	2	1
6. Hold position for 3 s.	3	2	1
Sum of column scores:			

Key to levels of assistance:

IND = Independent; the individual is able to perform the task without assistance.

PPA = Partial physical assistance; the individual needs some assistance to perform the task.

TPA = Total physical assistance; the individual needs assistance to perform the entire task.

Summary		Percentage of independence		
Total score achieved		6/18 = 33%	11/18 = 61%	16/18 = 88%
Total score possible	18	7/18 = 38%	12/18 = 66%	17/18 = 94%
% independent score		8/18 = 44%	13/18 = 72%	18/18 = 100%
Product score		9/18 = 50%	14/18 = 77%	
		10/18 = 55%	15/18 = 83%	

Modified from Houston-Wilson (1995).

A

BODY MASS INDEX CHART

Height (in)	49	51	53	55	57	59	61	63	65	67	69	71	73	75	77	79	81	83
Weight (lb)																		
66	19	18	16	15	14	13	12	12	11	10	10	9	9	8	8	8	7	7
70	20	19	18	16	15	14	13	13	12	11	10	10	9	9	8	8	8	7
75	22	20	19	17	16	15	14	13	12	12	11	10	10	9	9	9	8	8
79	23	21	20	18	17	16	15	14	13	12	12	11	11	10	9	9	9	8
84	24	22	21	19	18	17	16	15	14	13	12	12	11	11	10	10	9	9
88	26	24	22	20	19	18	17	16	15	14	13	12	12	11	11	10	10	9
92	27	25	23	21	20	19	17	16	15	15	14	13	12	12	11	11	10	10
97	28	26	24	22	21	20	18	17	16	15	14	14	13	12	12	11	10	10
101	29	27	25	23	22	20	19	18	17	16	15	14	13	13	12	12	11	10
106	31	28	26	24	23	21	20	19	18	17	16	15	14	13	13	12	11	11
110	32	30	27	26	24	22	21	20	18	17	16	15	15	14	13	13	11	11
114	33	31	29	27	25	23	22	20	19	18	17	16	15	14	14	13	12	12
119	35	32	30	28	26	24	22	21	20	19	18	17	16	15	14	14	13	12
123	36	33	31	29	27	25	23	22	21	19	18	17	16	16	15	14	13	13
128	37	34	32	30	28	26	24	23	21	20	19	18	17	16	15	15	14	13
132	38	36	33	31	29	27	25	23	22	21	20	19	18	17	16	15	14	14
136	40	37	34	32	29	28	26	24	23	21	20	19	18	17	16	16	15	14
141	41	38	35	33	30	28	27	25	24	22	21	20	19	18	17	16	15	15
145	42	39	36	34	31	29	27	26	24	23	22	20	19	18	17	17	16	15
150	44	40	37	35	32	30	28	27	25	24	22	21	20	19	18	17	16	15
154	45	41	38	36	33	31	29	27	26	24	23	22	20	19	18	18	17	16
158	46	43	40	37	34	32	30	28	26	25	24	22	21	20	19	18	17	16
163	47	44	41	38	35	33	31	29	27	26	24	23	22	20	19	19	18	17
167	49	45	42	39	36	34	32	30	28	26	25	23	22	21	20	19	18	17
172	50	46	43	40	37	35	32	30	29	27	25	24	23	22	21	20	19	18
176	51	47	44	41	38	36	33	31	29	28	26	25	23	22	21	20	19	18
180	52	49	45	42	39	36	34	32	30	28	27	25	24	23	22	21	20	19
185	54	50	46	43	40	37	35	33	31	29	27	26	25	23	22	21	20	19
189	55	51	47	44	41	38	36	34	32	30	28	27	25	24	23	22	20	20
194	56	52	48	45	42	39	37	34	32	30	29	27	26	24	23	22	21	20
198	58	53	49	46	43	40	37	35	33	31	29	28	26	25	24	23	21	20
202	59	54	50	47	44	41	38	36	34	32	30	28	27	25	24	23	22	21
207	60	56	52	48	45	42	39	37	35	33	31	29	27	26	25	24	22	21
211	61	57	53	49	46	43	40	38	35	33	31	30	28	27	25	24	23	22
216	63	58	54	50	47	44	41	38	36	34	32	30	29	27	26	25	23	22
220	64	59	55	51	48	44	42	39	37	35	33	31	29	28	26	25	24	23
224	65	60	56	52	49	45	42	40	37	35	33	31	30	28	27	26	24	23
229	67	62	57	53	49	46	43	41	38	36	34	32	30	29	27	26	25	24
233	68	63	58	54	50	47	44	41	39	37	35	33	31	29	28	27	25	24
238	69	64	59	55	51	48	45	42	40	37	35	33	32	30	28	27	26	24
242	70	65	60	56	52	49	46	43	40	38	36	34	32	30	29	28	26	25
246	72	66	61	57	53	50	47	44	41	39	37	35	33	31	29	28	27	25
251	73	67	63	58	54	51	47	45	42	39	37	35	33	32	30	29	27	26
255	74	69	64	59	55	52	48	45	43	40	38	36	34	32	31	29	28	26
260	76	70	65	60	56	52	49	46	43	41	39	36	34	33	31	30	28	27
264	77	71	66	61	57	53	50	47	44	42	39	37	35	33	32	30	29	27
268	78	72	67	62	58	54	51	48	45	42	40	38	36	34	32	31	29	28
273	79	73	68	63	59	55	52	48	46	43	40	38	36	34	33	31	30	28
277	81	75	69	64	60	56	52	49	46	44	41	39	37	35	33	32	30	29
282	82	76	70	65	61	57	53	50	47	44	42	40	37	35	34	32	30	29
286	83	77	71	66	62	58	54	51	48	45	42	40	38	36	34	33	31	29
290	84	78	72	67	63	59	55	52	48	46	43	41	39	37	35	33	31	30
295	86	79	74	68	64	60	56	52	49	46	44	41	39	37	35	34	32	30
299	87	80	75	69	65	60	57	53	50	47	44	42	40	38	36	34	32	31
304	88	82	76	70	66	61	57	54	51	48	45	43	40	38	36	35	33	31
308	90	83	77	71	67	62	58	55	51	48	46	43	41	39	37	35	33	32
312	91	84	78	72	68	63	59	55	52	49	46	44	41	39	37	36	34	32

Source: Panel on Energy, Obesity, and Body Weight Standards, 1987, *American Journal of Clinical Nutrition* Supplement 45 (5): 1035-47.

Purchasing and Constructing Unique Testing Supplies

Test item	Supply item	Resource address	Approximate cost	Phone
PACER (20 m and 16 m)	PACER tape	Cooper Institute for Aerobics Research 12330 Preston Rd. Dallas, TX 75230	$15.00	1-800-635-7050
Target aerobic movement test (TAMT)	Electronic heart rate monitor (many types are available)	Polar CIC, Inc. 370 Crossways Park Dr. Woodbury, NY 11797-2050	$159.00 for Polar PACER	1-800-290-6330
Skinfold test	Lange skinfold caliper	Beta Technology, Inc. 151 Harvey West Blvd. Santa Cruz, CA 95060	$196.00	1-408-426-5890
Back-saver sit and reach	Sit-and-reach Flex-Tester	Things from Bell P.O. Box 135 East Troy, WI 53120	$98.90	1-800-543-1457
Dominant grip strength	JAMAR grip dynamometer	Sammons Preston P.O. Box 5071 Bolingbrook, IL 60440	$189.95	1-800-323-5547
Seated push-up	Push-up blocks	Sammons Preston P.O. Box 5071 Bolingbrook, IL 60440	$98.00	1-800-323-5547

EQUIPMENT FOR BACK-SAVER SIT AND REACH

1. Using any sturdy wood or comparable material (3/4-in. [2-cm] plywood seems to work well) cut the following pieces:

   2 pieces—12 in. × 12 in. (30 cm × 30 cm)

   2 pieces—12 in. × 10.5 in. (30 cm × 26 cm)

   1 piece—12 in. × 22 in. (30 cm × 56 cm)

2. Cut pieces that are 10 in. × 4 in. (26 cm × 10 cm) from each corner of one end of the 12 in. × 22 in. piece to make the top of the box (see diagram). Beginning at the small end, make marks on the piece every inch (or centimeter) up to 12 in. (30 cm).

3. Construct a box using nails, screws, or wood glue from the remaining four pieces. Attach the top of the box. It is crucial that the 9-in. (23-cm) mark be exactly in line with the vertical plane against which the participant's foot will be placed. The zero mark is at the end that will be nearest to the participant.

4. Cover the apparatus with polyurethane sealer or shellac.

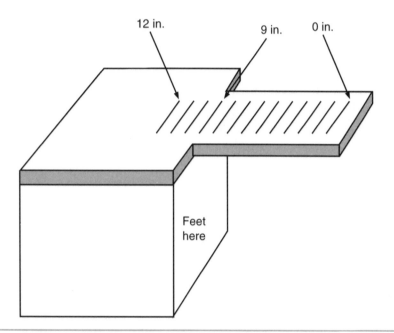

Figure B.1 Back-saver sit and reach apparatus.

Alternate Flexibility-Testing Apparatus

1. Find a sturdy cardboard box at least 12 in. (30 cm) tall. Turn the box so that the bottom is up. Tape a ruler or yardstick to the bottom. The yardstick must be placed so that the 9-in. (23-cm) mark is exactly in line with the vertical plane against which the participant's foot will be placed and the zero is nearer the participant.

2. Find a bench that is about 12 in. (30 cm) wide. Turn the bench on its side. Tape a ruler or yardstick to the bench so that the 9-in. (23-cm) mark is exactly in line with the vertical plane against which the participant's foot will be placed and the zero end is nearer the participant.

Information on this page was reprinted with permission from Cooper Institute for Aerobics Research, Dallas, Texas (1992).

EQUIPMENT FOR THE CONSTRUCTION OF A RAMP

Items needed

Ramp

1 ramp plywood, 3/4 in. × 36 in. × 96 in. (2 cm × 91 cm × 244 cm)

1 platform plywood, 3/4 in. × 36 in. × 48 in. (2 cm × 91 cm × 122 cm)

1 steel nosing, 1/2 in. × 3 in. × 36 in. (2 cm × 8 cm × 91 cm)

nails, wood screws, stove bolts

Ramp supports

3 pieces of wood for ramp plywood, 2 in. × (dimensions range from 0 in. to 7 1/2 in.) × 96 in. (5 cm × 19 cm × 244 cm)

1 piece of wood for platform plywood, 2 in. × 7 1/2 in. × 33 in. (5 cm × 19 cm × 82.5 cm)

1 piece of wood for platform plywood 2 in. × 3 3/4 in. × 33 in. (5 cm × 6.25 cm × 82.5 cm)

Rails

2 pieces of wood for ramp, 1 in. × (dimensions range from 2 in. to 10 in.) × 96 in. (2.5 cm × 25 cm × 244 cm)

1 piece of wood for platform, 1 in. × 10 in. × 48 in. (2.5 cm × 25 cm × 122 cm)

1 piece of wood for platform, 1 in. × 10 in. × 36 in. (2.5 cm × 25 cm × 91 cm)

Handles and brackets

6, 3 1/2 in. (9 cm) metal handles

2 pair, left-hand brackets

2 pair, right-hand brackets

Procedure

1. Cut out 1/2 in. (1 cm) deep × 3/4 in. (2 cm) back along the width of one end of the ramp plywood for steel nosing.
2. Drill four holes in plywood and steel nosing.
3. Apply steel nosing using four stove bolts.
4. Assemble ramp in one piece using 2 in. × (dimensions range from 0 in. to 7 1/2 in.) × 96 in. base supports running lengthwise under plywood 18 in. (45 cm) apart. Apply 3/4 in. × 36 in. × 96 in. ramp plywood over lengthwise supports using wood screws.
5. Assemble platform in the same way.

6. Cut ramp at 48 in. into two sections.

7. Apply 1 in. × (dimensions range from 2 in. to 10 in.) × 96 in. rails to sides of ramp after they have been cut in two to fit the dimensions of the ramp plywood.

8. Apply 1 in. × 10 in. × 48 in. and 1 in. × 10 in. × 36 in. rails to platform.

9. Apply two pair left side brackets and then two pair right side brackets to ramp. Brackets overlap to connect.

10. Apply a metal handle to the side of each platform and ramp section.

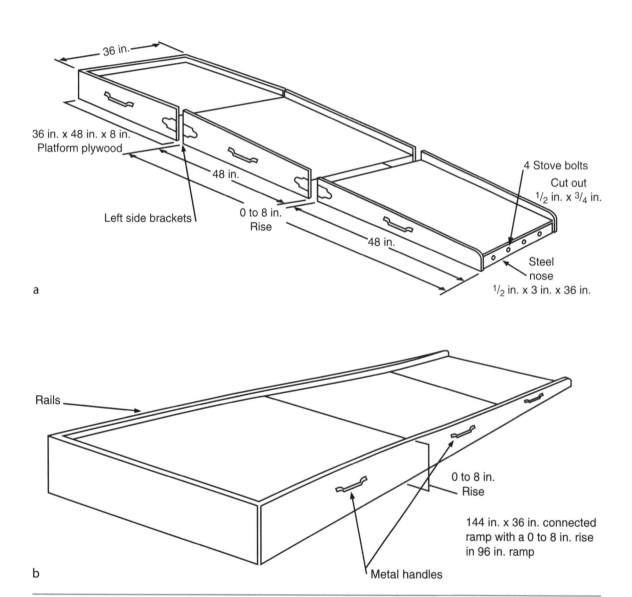

Figure B.2 Ramp and platform design plan: (*a*) disassembled; (*b*) assembled.

EQUIPMENT FOR MODIFIED PULL-UP

Items needed

1	3/4-in. (1 7/8-cm) plywood 24 in. × 39 in. (60 cm × 97 1/2 cm) for support platform
2	2 in. × 8 in. × 24 in. (5 cm × 20 cm × 60 cm) pieces for base of uprights
2	2 in. × 4 in. × 48 in. (5 cm × 10 cm × 120 cm) for uprights
1	1 1/8-in. (3 5/8-cm) steel pipe for chin-up bar
1	1 1/4-in. (3-cm) dowel for top support
24	3/8-in. (1-cm) dowel pieces cut 3 1/2 in. (8 3/4 cm) long
	nails, wood screws, and wood glue for construction

1. Drill a hole through the 2-in. width 2 1/2 in. (6 1/4 cm) from the top end of each of the 2 in. × 4 in. × 48 in. pieces for the 1 1/4-in. dowel support rod.
2. Drill eleven 1 1/8-in. holes below the first hole for the steel pipe. Measure 2 1/2 in. (6 1/4 cm) between the centers of these holes.
3. Beginning 3 3/4 in. (9 5/8 cm) from the top of these upright pieces, drill twelve 3/8-in. (1-cm) holes into the 4 in. width. Center these holes between the holes for the steel pipe.
4. Assemble the pieces and finish with polyurethane or shellac.

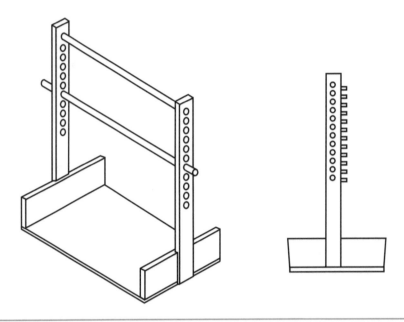

Figure B.3 Modified pull-up stand.

Information on this page was reprinted with permission from Cooper Institute for Aerobics Research, Dallas, Texas (1992).

C

Software Installation Instructions

INSTALLATION AND USE OF FITNESS CHALLENGE SOFTWARE

Install for Windows 95/98 Disk Installation

- Insert Fitness Challenge disk 1 into the a: or b: drive.
- Click the Windows 95/98 "Start" button.
- Click the "Run..." icon.
- Type "a:\setup.exe" or "b:\setup.exe" in the text box.
- Click the "OK" button.
- Follow the prompts to install the software.

Install for Windows 95/98 CD-ROM Installation

- Insert Fitness Challenge CD-ROM into the CD-ROM drive.
- Click the Windows 95/98 "Start" button.
- Click the "Run..." icon.
- Type "d:\setup.exe" or "e:\setup.exe" in the text box.
- Click the "OK" button.
- Follow the prompts to install the software.

Registering Fitness Challenge and Getting Started

- Click the Windows 95/98 "Start" button.
- Select the "Programs" folder icon.
- Select the "Fitness Challenge" folder icon.
- Click on the "Fitness Challenge" icon.
- At the next screen, enter the required information (*) to register Fitness Challenge. Press the "Register" button when you are finished.
- Your registration code will appear onscreen. Follow the instructions to receive your unlock code. *Note: Make sure the software is running when you call customer service.* The software will prompt you to call Human Kinetics to receive your unlock code. If you purchased the software outside the U.S., a sticker will be visible on the outside of the package informing you which HK subsidiary you should contact for your unlock code. If you should have any problems, call (217) 351-7051 or e-mail support@hkusa.com.
- Enter the unlock code to register Fitness Challenge and press the "Continue" button. Once this is done, you can start using the program.
- After Fitness Challenge is started, use online help to guide you through the program.

GLOSSARY

aerobic behavior—A subcomponent of aerobic functioning that relates to the ability to sustain physical activity of a specific intensity for a particular duration.

aerobic capacity—A subcomponent of aerobic functioning that relates to the highest rate of oxygen that can be consumed by a person while exercising.

aerobic functioning—The component of physical fitness that permits a person to sustain large-muscle, dynamic, moderate- to high-intensity activity for prolonged periods of time. Aerobic behavior and aerobic capacity are subcomponents of aerobic functioning.

body composition—The component of health-related physical fitness that is related to the degree of leanness or fatness of the body.

body mass index (BMI)—An index of the relationship between an individual's height and weight.

$$BMI = \frac{704.5 \times \text{body weight (lb.)}}{\text{height}^2 \text{ (in.)}} \quad \text{or} \quad \frac{\text{body weight (kg.)}}{\text{height}^2 \text{ (m)}}$$

components of physical fitness—Categories or constructs that measure separate or unique aspects of fitness. The health-related components of fitness adopted for the Brockport Physical Fitness Test include aerobic functioning, body composition, and musculoskeletal functioning.

criterion-referenced standard—A target measure of attainment against which a test score is judged. Criterion-referenced health standards used in the Brockport Physical Fitness Test are levels of attainment associated with physiological or functional health.

flexibility—A subcomponent of musculoskeletal functioning that reflects the extent of movement possible in multiple joints while performing a functional task.

functional health—An aspect of health related to the physical capability of the individual. Indices of functional health include the ability to perform important tasks independently, independently sustain the performance of those tasks, perform activities of daily living (ADLs), sustain physical activity, and participate in leisure activities.

general criterion-referenced standard—A target measure of attainment associated with a general population of youngsters or a standard that is not adjusted for the effects of impairment or disability. General standards may be recommended for youngsters with disabilities as well as for the general population.

health—"A human condition with physical, social, and psychological dimensions, each characterized on a continuum with positive and negative poles. Positive health is associated with a capacity to enjoy life and to withstand challenges; it is not merely the absence of disease. Negative health is associated with morbidity and, in the extreme, with premature mortality" (Bouchard & Shephard, 1994). In the

Brockport Physical Fitness Test, health is conceptualized as having both functional and physiological aspects.

health-related physical fitness—(a) An ability to perform and sustain daily activities and (b) demonstration of traits or capacities that are associated with a low risk of premature development of diseases and conditions related to movement. It refers to those components of fitness that are affected by habitual physical activity and relate to health status.

individualized standard—A desired level of attainment for an individual in an area of health status established in consideration of his or her present level of performance and expectation for progress. It may not necessarily reflect a health-related standard.

minimal standard—The lowest acceptable health-related, criterion-referenced level of attainment. Minimal general standards reflect minimally acceptable levels of health-related physical fitness for the general population.

muscular endurance—A subcomponent of musculoskeletal functioning that reflects the ability to repeatedly perform submaximal muscular contractions.

muscular strength—A subcomponent of musculoskeletal functioning that reflects the maximal amount of force that is exerted.

musculoskeletal functioning—The component of physical fitness that combines muscular strength, muscular endurance, and flexibility or range of motion.

optional test item—An alternative test item considered to be appropriate and acceptable for the measurement of components of physical fitness.

physical activity—Consists of any bodily movement produced by skeletal muscle resulting in a substantial increase over resting energy expenditure (Bouchard & Shephard, 1994).

physical fitness—A set of attributes that people have or achieve that relate to the ability to perform physical activity (Caspersen, Powell, & Christenson, 1985).

physiological health—An aspect of health related to organic well-being. Indices of physiological health include traits or capacities that are associated with well-being, absence of a disease or condition, or low risk of developing a disease or a condition.

preferred standard—A good health-related criterion-referenced level of attainment for the general population. A single general standard for a particular test item is considered equivalent to a preferred standard. Preferred general standards reflect good levels of health-related physical fitness for the general population.

profile—The direction or broad goal for a health-related physical fitness program.

range of motion—A subcomponent of musculoskeletal functioning that refers to the extent of movement in a single joint.

recommended test item—A test item considered to be appropriate and most acceptable for the measurement of physical fitness when factors for selecting test items are equal.

specific criterion-referenced standard—A target measure of attainment associated with a defined category of persons and/or a standard that is adjusted for the effects of impairment or disability. Specific standards are only provided for selected test items for specific target populations. They reflect minimal acceptable levels of health-related physical fitness adjusted for the effects of impairment.

References

American Association on Mental Retardation. (1992). *Mental retardation definition, classification, and systems of supports* (9th ed.). Washington, DC: American Association on Mental Retardation.

American College of Sports Medicine. (1990). The recommended quantity and quality of exercise for developing and maintaining cardiorespiratory and muscular fitness in health adults. *Medicine and Science in Sports and Exercise, 22*(2), 265-274.

American College of Sports Medicine. (1995). *ACSM's guidelines for exercise testing and prescription* (5th ed.). Media, PA: Williams & Wilkins.

Blair, S.N., Kohl, H.W., Gordon, N.F., & Paffenbarger, R.S., Jr. (1992). How much physical activity is good for health? *Annual Review Public Health, 13,* 99-126.

Blair, S.N., Kohl, H.W., Paffenbarger, R.S., Jr., Clark, D.G., Cooper, K.H., & Gibbons, L.W. (1989). Physical fitness and all-cause mortality: A prospective study of healthy men and women. *Journal of the American Medical Association, 262,* 931-933.

Blair, S.N., Kohl, H.W., Paffenbarger, R.S., Clark, D.G., Cooper, K.H., & Gibbons, L.W. (1990). Physical fitness and all-cause mortality: A prospective study of healthy men. *Journal of the American Medical Association, 262,* 2395-2401.

Bouchard, C., & Shephard, R.J. (1994). Physical activity, fitness, and health: The model and key concepts. In C. Bouchard, R.J. Shephard, & T. Stephens (Eds.), *Physical activity, fitness, and health international proceedings and consensus statement* (pp. 77-86). Champaign, IL: Human Kinetics.

Buell, C.E. (1983). *Physical education for blind children.* Springfield, IL: Charles C Thomas.

Caspersen, C.J., Powell, K.E., & Christenson, G.M. (1985). Physical activity, exercise, and physical fitness: Definitions and distinctions for health-related research. *Public Health Reports, 100,* 126-131.

Cerebral Palsy International Sport and Recreation Association. (1993). *CP-ISRA Handbook* (5th ed.). Heteren, Netherlands: Cerebral Palsy International Sport and Recreation Association.

Cole, T.M., & Tobis, J.S. (1990). Measurement of musculoskeletal function. In F.J. Kottke & J.F. Lehmann (Eds.), *Krusen's handbook of physical medicine and rehabilitation* (pp. 20-71). Philadelphia: Saunders.

Cooper Institute for Aerobics Research (CIAR). (1992). *The Prudential FITNESSGRAM test administration manual.* Dallas: Cooper Institute for Aerobics Research.

Cooper Institute for Aerobics Research (CIAR). (1999). *FITNESSGRAM test admininstration manual.* Champaign, IL: Human Kinetics.

Cureton, K.J. (1994a). Aerobic capacity. In J.R. Morrow, H.B. Falls, & H.W. Kohl (Eds.), *The Prudential FITNESSGRAM technical reference manual* (pp. 33-55). Dallas: Cooper Institute of Aerobics Research.

Cureton, K.J. (1994b). Physical fitness and activity standards for youth. In R.R. Pate & R.C. Hohn (Eds.), *Health and fitness through physical education* (pp. 129-136). Champaign, IL: Human Kinetics.

Cureton, K.J., & Warren, G.L. (1990). Criterion-referenced standards for youth health-related fitness tests: A tutorial. *Research Quarterly for Exercise and Sport, 61*(2), 7-19.

Daquila, G.A. (1982). *Reliability of selected health and performance related test items from the Project UNIQUE physical fitness inventory.* Unpublished master's thesis, State University of New York, College at Brockport.

Eichstaedt, C., & Lavay, B. (1992). *Physical activity for individuals with mental retardation.* Champaign, IL: Human Kinetics.

Eichstaedt, C., Polacek, J., Wang, P., & Dohrman, P. (1991). *Physical fitness and motor skill levels of individuals with mental retardation, ages 6-21.* Normal, IL: Illinois State University.

Fernhall, B., Pitetti, K., Vukavich, M., Stubbs, N., Hansen, T., Winnick, J., & Short, F. (1996). Validation of cardiovascular fitness field tests in children with mental retardation. *Medicine and Science in Sports and Exercise, 28*(Suppl. 2), 50.

Freedson, P.S. (1991). Electronic motion sensors and heart rate as measures of physical activity in children. *Journal of School Health, 61,* 220-223.

Freedson, P.S., & Melanson, E.L. (1996). Measuring physical activity. In D. Docherty (Ed.), *Measurement in pediatric exercise science* (pp. 261-283). Champaign, IL: Human Kinetics.

Government of Canada, Fitness and Amateur Sport. (1985). *Canada Fitness Award: Adapted for use by trainable mentally handicapped youth—a leader's manual* (rev. ed.). Ottawa, Ontario: Government of Canada, Fitness and Amateur Sport.

Hayden, F.J. (1964). *Physical fitness for the mentally retarded.* Toronto: Metropolitan Toronto Association for Retarded Children.

Houston-Wilson, C. (1995). Alternate assessment procedures. In American Association for Active Lifestyles and Fitness, *Physical best and individuals with disabilities: A handbook for inclusion in fitness programs* (pp. 91-95). Reston, VA: American Association for Active Lifestyles and Fitness.

Jansma, P., Decker, J., Ersing, W., McCubbin, J., & Combs, S. (1988). A fitness assessment system for individuals with severe mental retardation. *Adapted Physical Activity Quarterly, 5,* 223-232.

Jéquier, Eric. (1987). Energy, obesity, and body weight standards. *American Journal of Clinical Nutrition, 45,* 1035.

Jette, M., Sidney, K., & Cicutti, N. (1984, September-October). A critical analysis of sit-ups: A case for the partial curl-up as a test for abdominal muscular endurance. *Canadian Association of Health, Physical Education, and Recreation Journal,* pp. 4-9.

Johnson, R.E., & Lavay, B. (1989). Fitness testing for children with special needs: An alternative approach. *Journal of Physical Education, Recreation, and Dance, 60*(6), 50-53.

Kosiak, M., & Kottke, F.J. (1990). Prevention and rehabilitation of ischemic ulcers. In F.J. Kottke & J.F. Lehmann (Eds.), *Krusen's handbook of physical medicine and rehabilitation* (pp. 976-987). Philadelphia: Saunders.

Leger, L.A., Mercier, D., Gadoury, C., & Lambert, J. (1988). The multistage 20 metre shuttle run test for aerobic fitness. *Journal of Sports Sciences, 6,* 93-101.

Lohman, T.G. (1992). *Advances in body composition assessment.* Champaign, IL: Human Kinetics.

Lohman, T.G. (1994). Body composition. In J.R. Morrow, H.B. Falls, & H.W. Kohl (Eds.), *The Prudential FITNESSGRAM technical reference manual* (pp. 57-72). Dallas: Cooper Institute of Aerobics Research.

McArdle, W.D., Katch, F.I., & Katch V.L. (1994). *Essentials of exercise physiology.* Philadelphia: Lea & Febiger.

Paffenbarger, R.S., Jr., & Lee, I-M. (1996). Physical activity and fitness for health and longevity. *Research Quarterly for Exercise and Sport, 67*(Suppl. 3).

Pate, R.R. (1988). The evolving definition of fitness. *Quest, 40,* 174-178.

Pate, R.R., Pratt, M., Blair, S.N., Haskell, W.L., Macera, C.A., Bouchard, C., Buchner, D., Ettinger, W., Heath, G.W., King, A.C., Kriska, A., Leon, A.S., Marcus, B.H., Morris, J., Paffenbarger, R.S., Patrick, K., Pollack, M.L., Rippe, J.M., Sallis, J., & Wilmore, J.H. (1995). Physical activity and public health. *Journal of the American Medical Association, 273*(5), 402-407.

Patterson, P., Wiksten, D.L., Ray, L., Flanders, C., & Sanphy, D. (1996). The validity and reliability of the back saver sit and reach test in middle school girls and boys. *Research Quarterly for Exercise and Sport, 67,* 448-451.

Plowman, S.A., & Corbin, C.B. (1994). Muscular strength, endurance, and flexibility. In J.R. Morrow, H.B. Falls, & H.W. Kohl (Eds.), *The Prudential FITNESSGRAM technical reference manual* (pp. 73-100). Dallas: Cooper Institute of Aerobics Research.

President's Council on Physical Fitness and Sports. (1996). Physical activity and health: A report of the Surgeon General. *Physical Activity and Fitness Research Digest, 2*(6).

Project Target Advisory Committee. (1997, April 18-19). Meeting of the Project Target Advisory Committee, Brockport, NY.

Rimmer, J.H., Connor-Kuntz, F., Winnick, J.P., & Short, F.X. (1997). Feasibility of the target aerobic movement test in children and adolescents with spina bifida. *Adapted Physical Activity Quarterly, 14,* 147-155.

Robertson, L.D., & Magnusdottir, H. (1987). Evaluation of criteria associated with abdominal fitness testing. *Research Quarterly for Exercise and Sport, 58,* 355-359.

Safrit, M.J., & Wood, T.M. (1995). *Introduction to measurement in physical education and exercise science* (3rd ed.). St. Louis: Mosby.

Shephard, R.J. (1990). *Fitness in special populations.* Champaign, IL: Human Kinetics.

Shephard, R.J. (1994). *Aerobics fitness and health.* Champaign, IL: Human Kinetics.

Short, F.X., & Winnick, J.P. (1999). *The Fitness Challenge: Software for the Brockport Physical Fitness Test* [computer software]. Champaign, IL: Human Kinetics.

U.S. Department of Health and Human Services. (1996). *Physical activity and health: A report of the Surgeon General.* Atlanta: U.S. Department of Health and Human Services, Centers for Disease Control and Prevention, National Center for Chronic Disease Prevention and Health Promotion.

Waters, R.L. (1992). Energy expenditure. In J. Perry, *Gait analysis: Normal and pathological function* (pp. 443-487). Thorofare, NJ: Slack.

Winnick, J.P., & Short, F.X. (1982). *The physical fitness of sensory and orthopedically impaired youth: Project UNIQUE final report.* Brockport, NY: State University of New York.

Winnick, J.P., & Short, F.X. (1985). *Physical fitness testing of the disabled: Project UNIQUE.* Champaign, IL: Human Kinetics.

Winnick, J.P., & Short, F.X. (1998). *Criterion-referenced physical fitness standards for adolescents with disabilities: Project Target final report.* Brockport, NY: State University of New York.

Index

Contributors

Central Staff at the State University of New York, College at Brockport

Project Director:	Joseph P. Winnick
Project Coordinator:	Francis X. Short
	George Lawther (1993-94)
Graduate Assistants:	Kevin Biata
	Mary Powers
	Rob Korzeniewski
	Kevin Wexler
	Lori Erickson

Office of Special Education and Rehabilitative Services

Project Officer: Melville Appell

Project Target Advisory Committee and Panel of Experts

Kirk J. Cureton, PhD, University of Georgia
Harold W. Kohl, PhD, Baylor Sports Medicine Institute
Kenneth Richter, DO, medical director, U.S. Cerebral Palsy Athletic Association
James H. Rimmer, PhD, Northern Illinois University
Margaret Jo Safrit, PhD, American University
Roy J. Shephard, MD, PhD, DPE (retired), University of Toronto
Julian U. Stein, EdD (retired), George Mason University

Consultants

Patrick DiRocco	University of Wisconsin-La Crosse
Bo Fernhall	George Washington University
Georgia Frey	Texas Tech University
Timothy G. Lohman	University of Arizona
Jeffrey McCubbin	Oregon State University
Paul Surburg	Indiana University

Field Testers

Dianne Agostinelli	Karenne Bloomgarden
Tim Baird	Carol Brun Del Re
Matthew Beaty	Ed Carll
Ron Berman	Mary Coe
Kevin Biata	Fiona Connor-Kuntz
Kelly Bissell	Tim Coyle
Joel Blakeman	Ben Drake

Kelda DePrez
Kathryn Efthimiades
Bo Fernhall
Deborah Follis
Jean Friedel
Ellen Gill
Gerard Gonsalves
Victoria Gross
Terri Hansen
David Haveman
Wendy Kohler
Robert Korzeniewski
Shelly Kron
Lauren Lieberman
Tosha Litwinski
Laura Mauer
Nancy McNulty
Alayne Miller
Stephen O'Hanlon
Kenneth Pitetti
Travis Phillips
Elizabeth Pitts

Mary Powers
Dana Rieger
James Rimmer
Maria Rodriguez
Amy Roska
Laura Scala
David Seefeldt
Michelle Shea
Steve Skaggs
Louis Stadler
Eric Stern
Nancy Stubbs
Mary Szekely
Cindy Thomas
Lori Volding
Matthew Vukovich
Mary Walsh
Kevin Wexler
Stephanie White
Matthew Wilkins
Melissa Zurlo

Other Contributors

Val Benzing, Brockport, NY
Jean Berry, Brockport, NY
Dixie Butler, Brockport, NY
Michael Coriale, Brockport, NY
Mel Eisenback, New York, NY
Robert Ellis, Brockport, NY
Arnie Epstein, New York, NY
Sister Seraphine Herbst, Rochester, NY
Jack Hogan, Brockport, NY
Sam Hughes, Houston Independent School District
Pat Johnson, Brockport, NY
Bob Jones, Brockport, NY
Brian Jones, Brockport, NY
Richard Kingdon, Brockport, NY
Robert Lewis, New York, NY
Pam Maryjanowski, Empire State Games for the Physically Challenged
Gregory Packard, Brockport, NY
Fred Parker, Brockport, NY
Paul Ponchillia, Michigan Blind Athletic Association
Jack Purificato, Brockport, NY
Joseph Setak, Brockport, NY
Pam Siedlecki, Brockport, NY
William Straub, Ithaca, NY
Wendy Wheeler, Brockport, NY

Testing Projects

Brockport Central School District	Brockport, NY
George Washington University Project	Washington, DC
Houston Independent School District	Houston, TX
Michigan State School for the Blind	Lansing, MI
New York City Public Schools	New York, NY
Empire State Games for the Physically Challenged	Brockport, NY
Northern Illinois University Project	DeKalb, IL
Oregon State University	Corvallis, OR
School of the Holy Childhood	Rochester, NY
Western Michigan University	Kalamazoo, MI
Paralympic Games	Atlanta, GA

About the Authors

Joseph P. Winnick, EdD, is a professor of physical education and sport at the State University of New York, College at Brockport. He received master's and doctoral degrees from Temple University. Dr. Winnick developed and implemented America's first master's degree professional preparation program in adapted physical education at Brockport in 1968 and since that time has secured funds from the U.S. Department of Education to support the program. He has and continues to be involved in research related to the physical fitness of persons with disabilities. He is the editor of *Adapted Physical Education and Sport, Second Edition* (Human Kinetics 1995). Dr. Winnick has received the G. Lawrence Rarick Research Award and the Hollis Fait Scholarly Contribution Award.

Francis X. Short, PED, is associate professor and chair of the Department of Physical Education and Sport at State University of New York, College at Brockport. Dr. Short has been involved with adapted physical education programs for the past 25 years. He has coauthored numerous journal articles related to physical fitness and youngsters with disabilities. He is coauthor of *Physical Fitness Testing of the Disabled* (Human Kinetics 1985) and author of "Physical Fitness," a chapter in *Adapted Physical Education and Sport*. He has served as project coordinator for three federally funded research projects pertaining to physical fitness and youngsters with disabilities. Dr. Short is a member of the American Alliance for Health, Physical Education, Recreation and Dance and the National Consortium on Physical Education and Recreation for Individuals with Disabilities.

Related Resources

THE BROCKPORT PHYSICAL FITNESS TEST KIT

Joseph P. Winnick, EdD and Francis X. Short, PED
1999 • CD-ROM for Windows • 3.5" disk for Windows

The test kit contains the three items below and the test manual, plus curl-up strips, skinfold calipers, and the PACER audiocassette and CD. The kit provides users with what they need to accurately assess fitness levels and to help students improve their fitness levels.

FITNESS CHALLENGE

Joseph P. Winnick, EdD and Francis X. Short, PED
1999 • 3.5" diskettes

The companion software that makes using the Brockport Test much easier.

THE BROCKPORT PHYSICAL FITNESS TEST ADMINISTRATION VIDEO (APPROX 30-MINUTE VIDEOTAPE)

Joseph P. Winnick, EdD and Francis X. Short, PED
1999 • VHS

Demonstrates clearly how to use the Brockport Physical Fitness Test for youths with physical and mental disabilities.

THE BROCKPORT PHYSICAL FITNESS TRAINING GUIDE

Joseph P. Winnick, EdD and Francis X. Short, PED
1999 • Paperback • Approx 200 pp

Designed to help teachers create programs for students who need to improve in one or more areas of fitness as identified by the test.

To request more information or to order, U.S. customers call 1-800-747-4457, e-mail us at **humank@hkusa.com**, or visit our Web site at **http://www.humankinetics.com/**. Persons outside the U.S. can contact us via our Web site or use the appropriate telephone number, postal address, or e-mail address shown in the front of this book.

The American Fitness Alliance

The Brockport Physical Fitness Test and Fitness Challenge software are offered through The American Fitness Alliance (AFA), a collaborative effort of AAHPERD, the Cooper Institute for Aerobics Research (CIAR), and Human Kinetics. AFA offers additional assessment resources, which can be combined with those listed above to create a complete health-related physical education program:

- The *FITNESSGRAM* test for evaluating students' physical fitness, developed by CIAR
- The *Physical Best Program*, which identifies the components of successful health-related physical education and provides the material needed to implement it in classes
- *FitSmart*, the first national test designed to assess high school students' knowledge of concepts and principles of physical fitness

 HUMAN KINETICS
The Information Leader in Physical Activity